If You...

Really

Want to Live,

Be Extraordinary!

A 21st Century Guide to
Practicing Christian Living

Jo Lena Johnson
Dr. Lee Roy Jefferson

MISSION POSSIBLE PRESS
Creating Legacies through Absolute Good Works
www.jolenajohnson.com
www.BeExtraordinaryBook.com

The Mission is Possible.
Sharing love and wisdom for the young and "the young at heart,"
expanding minds,
restoring kindness through
good thoughts, feelings, and attitudes
is our intent.
May you thrive and be good in all you are and all you do…
Be Cause U.R. Absolute Good!

Scripture quotations are from *The Holy Bible, The New Open Bible Study Edition (KJV)* © 1990 by Thomas Nelson, Inc.

Other Scriptural References are from Biblegateway.com (New International Version).

If You Really Want to Live, Be Extraordinary! A 21st Century Guide to Practicing Christian Living

ISBN 978-0-9827520-0-5

Published by Mission Possible Press. Logos and marks are trademarks of the publisher. For information, contact Absolute Good Training & Life Skills Management at training@absolutegood.com.

We dedicate this book to each person who really wants to live a different life. It is possible with precision, dedicated effort, and God.

To my remarkable wife, Jeanette, an amazing professional registered nurse with incredible nursing skills and dedication to patient care. To my two wonderful children, Erica Jefferson Gamble, and Byron Lee Jefferson. To my two loving parents the late Waverly and Eula Jefferson, and my siblings Barbara (deceased), Joseph, Isaac, Delbert, Waverly, Jr., and Alma, whose words and inspiration still guide me.

—Dr. Lee Roy Jefferson

To each of my parents—my dynamic and lovely mother, Sandy (Johnson) McHugh; to Kenneth and Vera Johnson; to Bill and Alice McHugh; and to my brother William, Jr.—Thank you for all that you are, all that you do, and all that you continue to give. I am humbled to know you and honored to be family.

Father-God, Thank You. May each person touched by these works receive some of Your preciousness as a result.

—Jo Lena Johnson

OUR MISSION: PUTTING GOOD IN THE UNIVERSE

Dr. Lee Roy Jefferson has a lot to share. I believe your life will be enriched and fortified by his life and message. He is a son, brother, husband, father, and a good friend. As a "best educator" and "messenger," he is a man of integrity, honor, and kindness. He cares about people and is committed to the process and protocol of education. I've also found him to be quite charming and funny. While working with him to produce this work, I have been encouraged, strengthened, and taught things I didn't know, things I didn't remember, and things that I *really* want everyone to know.

You will hear directly from Dr. Jefferson in his own words as he told shared with me during our interview. Later in the book, we switch formats wherein I include the questions I asked and his answers. You will also meet nearly thirty friends whom we believe will touch your life—and who have some things they *really* want to share with you.

May you find these pages to be helpful on your quest to become educated on the most important subject there ever was and ever will be. Our intent is to introduce purpose-driven principles, steps, and ultimately, scripture that will lead you to a place of peace, rest, and salvation. The True Book, the Good Book, *The Holy Bible* addresses every care and concern for all of us—if we have access, the ability to read or listen, and an understanding of what is being said.

God, the Holy Father, teaches people and, as a true believer, so does Dr. Jefferson while fulfilling his purpose in life as a Christian educator, man of God, and author.

Jo Lena Johnson, Founder & Publisher
Mission Possible Press

FOREWORD

In this post modern era there is a great need for biblical direction. Some spiritual leaders have given in to proclaiming a philosophical perspective devoid of biblical truth. Lee Roy Jefferson and Jo Lena Johnson have provided the contemporary Christian reader with a practical book evolving from the Word of God.

From the deck of a cruise liner, I looked into the Caribbean ocean and saw pieces of driftwood being whirled about and bumped along by the waves of a deep blue ocean. As we pulled away from the harbor, I saw sailing vehicles of many shapes, sizes, and styles—from the small Jet Ski to the large naval cruisers. They differ vastly from the driftwood. They had clarity of purpose, a sense of direction, a source of power, and a consistent responsibility. Too many people in the body of Christ and in the world are floaters. Jefferson and Johnson's book is a great vehicle to help us put God's Word into action, so that we achieve meaningful moments and well spent lives.

God did not create us to be floaters. He did not choose us in Christ to be driftwood. Jefferson and Johnson provide everyday practical biblically based steps to be "extraordinary." What is wonderful about this book is that it is applicable to any person at any point in their life. The vast compilation of contributors delightfully produces creative and innovative directives to avoid just floating through life. This powerful resource ought to be used for those who are in the early formative stages of their life so that they can avoid wasting the valuable resources God has given them.

While this book is extremely helpful and useful for any person at any stage in life, I pray that Youth Leaders, young people, Pastors, and teachers would read this book and share it with those persons that they are guiding to live meaningful lives for the glory of God.

In The Bonds of the Spirit,
Dr. George W. Waddles, Sr., Pastor
Zion Hill Missionary Baptist Church, Chicago, Illinois;
President of the National Baptist Convention USA, Inc.
Congress of Christian Education

Share with Us

We would be honored to hear your thoughts and activities in response to this book. Let us know what your favorite portions are and how they affect you or your life.

Meet Us

We invite you to share your projects and efforts to "put good in the Universe," whether the efforts are personal stories from home, large-scale projects in your community, or a force that has beamed around the globe.

We teach, we speak, and we travel to connect with people—conducting training sessions, workshops, and classes to help tell stories, build legacies, and to learn more ways to focus on the extraordinary purpose of others.

Contribute Good, Too

This book is the first of four books in the "*If You Really Want to…*" series. With each book, at least 20% of sales go toward putting more good in the universe by supporting tangible projects and generating good work. Working together, we can create more resources, more wisdom, more access, and support more young people. Creating good together blesses everyone.

Contact Us Today. Email at: Goodworks@absolutegood.com or visit www.jolenajohnson.com.

Table of Contents

PREFACE Our Mission—Putting Good in the
Universe. v

FOREWORD by Dr. George Waddles, Sr. vii

SHARE WITH US ix

SECTION ONE: THE PAST AND YOUR NEW EXTRAORDINARY

Chapter 1. Reflections: Family, Community,
and Church Life. 1

Chapter 2. Seven Keys to Extraordinary
Christian Living. 4

SECTION TWO: ASSISTING PEOPLE

Chapter 3. Guidance for People. 13

Chapter 4. Guidance on Family. 20
A Father's Tale—Valuing the Breath of Life,
Dr. Edwin Bailey, Jr. 25
A Mother's Pride and Love: Sacrifices and Blessings,
Alice Grey. 34
Getting into Mom Mode: Wisdom Simply Spoken,
Daryle Glynn Brown. 37

Chapter 5. Guidance on Education. 38
"Thrusting, Bragging…:" A Message to Teachers and Parents,
Vera Raglin (Veteran Educator) 41
Education, Choices, and Military Service,
Chris Bynote (Young, Single, Christian Male) 50

SECTION THREE: SHINING BRIGHTLY AND EVERYDAY LIVING

Chapter 6. Seven Ways to Show
Your Brilliance 55

Chapter 7. Demonstrating Brilliance 64
A Model for Responsibility, Chief Sherman George 65
A Jazzy Legacy, Dwayne D. Bosman 69
Smiling Works! Christopher Cannon. 74
Be Winners, Not Quitters, Ni-Rita Baker-Bradford. 78
From Magna Cum Laude to Corporate Leadership,
Cecil W. Johnson, III 83
Hollywood and The Urban Buzz, Kevin Fleming 88
A Collegiate Journey to the NFL, Daryl E. Whittington. ... 93

SECTION FOUR: CHURCH LIFE—INSIDE THE WALLS

Chapter 8. Behaving as a Minister 97

Chapter 9. Keys to Building a
Successful Ministry 103
A Passion for Good Customer Service, Dawn Conner 108

Chapter 10. Engage People 113
Three Practical Reasons to Attend Church,
Pastor Damon Cannon 120

Chapter 11. Serving in the Church 121
Five Things I Love about My Church, Arlene Gibbs 121
Loyal Service, Elder Evelyn E. Murden. 124
Responsible Service, Ben Broadnax. 129

Chapter 12. Messages from Young Ministers..... 132
Things I Really Want Pioneering Church Leaders
to Know, Reverend Kevin Ross 132
Churchianity, God, and Chicken Dinners,
Pastor Cedric Portis. 136

SECTION FIVE: ACTION TO EXTRAORDINARY DAILY LIVING

Chapter 13. Context—Figuring Out What
You Really Want............................ 144
Your Journey...Depends on Your Roadmap! 144
Defining Conflict 148

Chapter 14. Leadership: Establishing Your
Priorities 154
The Five Main Areas of Living.................... 154
Living as a Leader: Questions and Considerations....... 158
7 Leadership Activities 160

Chapter 15. Legacy: Establishing Your Lasting
Value 161
Fitness and Good Health, Afua Bromley, L.Ac 169
Creating the Children's Dental Zone,
Dr. Candace Wakefield 176
From Dallas to Wall Street, Zachary K. Hawkins 179
Team, Works, Martin Luther Mathews 183
Building Relationships, Professor Clyde C. Ruffin 188

Chapter 16. Faith and Communication
Considerations 191
Business Blessings, Gail Day..................... 193
Forgiveness is Not an Option; It Is Required,
Reverend William H. Knight..................... 200

Chapter 17. Conflict, Sam, and Living
Extraordinarily............................. 209
Connecting Good People—Email to Kevin Fleming and
Daryl Whittington 210
Cotton Pickin' Leadership—Maida Coleman 217

Chapter 18. Resources for You to Take Action!... 220
YOUR MISSION IS POSSIBLE!................... 223
"God Can Use Anyone," Dr. Robert C. Scott.......... 232
Simple Things about Banking/Finance,
Michelle Brown 242

Chapter 19. My Life and More
Dr. Lee Roy Jefferson 248

**Chapter 20. Thank God for My Unique Blend
of Family, Friends, and Mentors**
Jo Lena Johnson 257

APPENDIX—SERMONS AND BOOKS

*"Brokenness: God's Equation to Fruitful Living!"
Minister Daryl E. Whittington* 285
"Hope for the Hurting," Pastor Cedric Portis. 292
Recommended Resources, Dr. Lee Roy Jefferson 301

SECTION ONE: REMEMBERING THE PAST AND CREATING YOUR OWN MODERN REALITY

Chapter 1

Reflections of Family, Community, and Church Life
Dr. Lee Roy Jefferson

"Love must be sincere. Hate what is evil; Cling to what is good.
Be devoted to one another in brotherly love.
Honor one another above yourselves.
Never be lacking in zeal, but keep your
spiritual fervor, serving the Lord.
Be joyful in hope, patient in affliction, and faithful in prayer.
Share with God's people who are in need. Practice Hospitality."
Romans 12:9–13 (NIV)

I made my entry at the Caney Valley Hospital with Dr. Martin at 3:30 a.m. on November 18, 1945…

I was brought up in Wharton, Texas, and raised to have a strong belief in God, Family, and Service. God had been dealing with my life, and I had been doing everything I could do NOT to become a minister. In my reluctance and rebellion, I became ill. Out of that context, God called me, and I became a minister at a young age.

1

One day, at the age of 13, I was cutting the lawn and began to feel faint. I was able to turn the lawn mower off before becoming unconscious. I'm still unclear about the actual diagnosis; however, "something" came over me, and I was in the hospital for 4 days. I knew it was by the blessing and miracle of God that I lived. From that experience, I said to Him, "God, I will preach your Word." I've been doing so ever since.

At that time, "the church" was more spiritual, more religious. "Obedience to God" was the foundation for the teaching and for the expectation of behavior for young people, for parents, and for the church. The churches supported the community and the community supported the churches. It was also an environment wherein people looked out for each other and their children.

The central person in each family was the mother—the person guiding and watching over. Mothers and grandmothers were strong in character and strong anchors. Core values of service, integrity, hard work, and clear expectations, including treating each other right, loving each other, and helping each other. "What's yours is mine and what's mine is yours" were not only taught, they were demonstrated. People didn't charge for childcare; people just took care of each other. If you had to go to the doctor, or needed to go to a meeting, and had to be away for the day or a couple of days, people would watch over each other. That environment brought forth many young men into the Gospel.

So, becoming an actual licensed minister took some time and effort...

Soon after my stay in the hospital, I met with the Pastor Reverend E. S. Fields of my church, Rising Star Baptist Church, (which is today, Camp Zion Rising Star Baptist Church), in Wharton, Texas.

Following that conference, on the second Sunday of March, five years after I was baptized and became a Christian in the church, I acknowledged "my call" like one who comes up and joins the church. I told the pastor and the congregation that I was coming forward because God had led me to become a minister of His Gospel, that I had made the commitment to be a minister of the Gospel of Jesus Christ which includes preaching and teaching. Then the pastor accepted me and my acknowledgment of my call, and the congregation accepted and supported me as a young minister in the Gospel.

Because of my age, I spent years under the Pastor's tutelage—whatever he would ask me to do or delegate me to do, that's what I did. I worked closely in assisting the Pastor in presiding and assisting in worship—sometimes it was reading scripture, sometimes it was leading prayer, and sometimes it was being a worshipper and observer. I would sometimes be in the front or second row of the church, where the deacons or leaders sit—*sometimes*; near the pulpit or in the pulpit…it just depended on what was happening at the time and the types of activities that day.

I had a rough childhood because once I became a minister, I couldn't go to a dance, to a football game, or to the movies, since people believed that, as a minister, I could not participate in those types of environments. I was in the south, the "Bible Belt." This affected every aspect of my life and liberties, in terms of belief and obedience. Also, during this period, ministers did not rush to give a license to a young preacher as, I Timothy 5:22 says, "*Endorse no man suddenly, neither be a partner in other men's sins: keep thyself pure.*" I was only considered a "young preacher."

I made it through junior high and high school and, eventually, Pastor gave me the ministerial license five years after acknowledging my call.

Chapter 2

Seven Keys to Extraordinary Christian Living
Dr. Lee Roy Jefferson

"Do not conform any longer to the pattern of this world, but be transformed by the renewing of your mind. Then you will be able to test and approve what God's Will is. His good, pleasing and perfect will."
Romans 12:2 (NIV)

It is impossible to end up successful and surprised at the same time. Extraordinary Living and Effective Education is not an accident, but it is the result of sustained effort. That is a fact. The following are *Seven Keys* that will aid you in developing, growing, and sustaining an "Effective Christian Education."

Extraordinary: Notably unusual or exceptional.
Christian Living: Practices, habits, and
principles applied to your life based on the
greatest book ever written, The Holy Bible.
Leader = You

Key #1: Enjoy Your Present.

This present moment should be completely experienced. Your day should be savored, not gulped down. Your life is a precious gift from God. Don't run through it. Yesterday is in the womb and tomorrow is in the tomb. Today is *really* the only place you'll ever be. All you have is today. You don't even have a future because when you arrive there you will rename it…today. Enjoy your gift of today, as it is truly your present.

> *"This is the day which the Lord hath made;*
> *we will rejoice and be glad in it."*
> Psalm 118:24

Happiness is always in the "now." It is not in the future. If you do not know how to enjoy the today that exists, you probably will not enjoy any day in your future. Jesus' entire ministry lasted about 1,000 days. He made every day count through precise living. Live today with precision. Precision in the present produces preeminence in the future.

> *"Show me someone who does a good job, and I*
> *will show you someone who is better than most*
> *and worthy of the company of kings."*
> Proverbs 22:29 (GNT)

Key #2: Sit at the Feet of the Best (Mentorship).

What is impossible to one man is the norm for another. It is essential that you find a worthy mentor, someone who is accustomed to success. Make it your goal to learn from the very best qualified mentors who will provoke quantum leaps forward in your life. Don't under estimate this truth; it is the key to exponential growth.

> *"Remember your leaders, who spoke the word*
> *of God to you. Consider the outcome of their*
> *way of life and imitate their faith."*
> Hebrews 13:7 (NIV)

If you want to improve your golf game, you must play with someone who is better than you are. In life, what could take ten years will happen in five, if you choose qualified mentors. You will save time and a lot of money because they will teach you how to see the world differently. Your friends are comfortable with the way you are, your mentors care about you too much to leave you that way. Pursue a worthwhile mentor.

> *"Obey your leaders and submit to their authority. They keep watch over you as men who must give an account. Obey them so that their work will be a joy, not a burden, for that would be of no advantage to you."*
> Hebrews 13:17 (NIV)

Key #3: Update Your Goals.

Your goals will change as you do. Your present feelings are not permanent, nor are your present circumstances. One day you will look back at the goals you presently have and be amazed at how you have changed.

> *"You have persevered and have endured hardships for my name, and have not grown weary."*
> Revelation 2:3 (NIV)

Goal setting is not a one-time event, but rather a gradual revelation of your purpose. You will go through different experiences that will shape and enhance your outlook. You must continuously assess and evaluate where you are and make the necessary adjustments. Effective people, educators, and leaders allow their goals to grow with them.

"Do you not know that in a race, all the runners run, but only
one gets the prize? Run in such a way as to get the prize."
I Corinthians 9:24

Key #4: Be Yourself.

You are one-of-a-kind. Your experiences, personality, background, and talents, make you unique.

"One God and Father of all, who is above
all, and through all, and in you all."
Ephesians 4:6

Each person has a calling, a purpose, and a divine plan available. There is no replica of you. There is no carbon copy of you. There is no mold of you on file. Don't expect everyone to accept your style and don't insult God by trying to be something else.

"...To equip God's people to do his work and
build up the church, the body of Christ."
Ephesians 4:12 (NLT)

Whether at work or leading a family, produce your best works by being reliable, becoming skilled, wise, and aware because you teach others how to behave, whether you realize it or not. Everyone will not necessarily like you, appreciate you, or choose to be in your space. The way we are in unity is that each person contributes to the whole. Whatever falls your lot...Be yourself. In the words of E.E. Cummings, "Be nobody but yourself in a world which is trying its best to make you like everybody else."

If you desire to be, or are already in the ministry, being yourself is one of the greatest depths that you can take towards being an effective minister. Effective ministers know and accept that many will not respond to their ministry. Some people would not cross the street to hear you while others would fly from another country. You are not assigned to everybody; you are assigned to somebody. Don't expect everyone to accept your style of ministry, and don't insult God by trying to make yourself into something that you are not. God knows what He is doing. So, show that you trust Him by living out your God-given originality.

> *"…for we are God's masterpiece." He has created us anew in Christ Jesus, so we can do the good things he planned for us long ago."*
> Ephesians 2:8–10 (NLT)

Key #5: Think Big.

Take the limits off your thinking. The key is exposure. A mind that once stretched for a new idea can never return to its previous state. A mind not exposed to a new idea can never grow. The Bible is the source of God's Word—use it, live it, and connect with it in Spirit.

> *"Do not let this Book of the Law depart from your mouth; meditate on it day and night, so that you may be careful to do everything written in it. Then you will be prosperous and successful."*
> Joshua 1:8 (NIV)

You can be an effective leader, parent, educator, or minister, by cultivating the ability to routinely see things that are invisible to others, by constantly exposing yourself to new information. Share wisdom at least as frequently as you eat every meal. Effective leaders become that way because of the way they see things.

Peter was walking on water, following Jesus' command, and he saw the winds and began to sink. Then Jesus reached out his hand and caught him. It is up to you, in your position of leadership—personally, professionally, or in the ministry, to see things differently than the average person.

Opportunities are only available to the trained eye. There are worlds of opportunities that presently surround you. The question is whether you can see them or not. Jesus tells us:

> *"And all things, whatsoever ye shall ask in*
> *prayer, believing, ye shall receive."*
> Matthew 21:22

Key #6: Create Order.

Order is the accurate arrangement of things: Order is placing things where they belong in your life, family, career, and ministry.

Order is a lifestyle: Each act of your life either increases or decreases order. You should view your life as a whole system in which everything affects everything else.

Disorder causes confusion and opens you up to negative consequences.

> *"For though I am absent from you in body, I am*
> *present with you in spirit and delight to see how orderly*
> *you are and how firm your faith in Christ is."*
> Colossians 2:5 (NIV)

Have you ever misplaced your car keys? You lost valuable time and emotional energy searching everywhere, even in places where you know they could not be. You ended up agitated and angry. It affects your life until they are found. In this same way a missed phone call here, a file out of order there, will destroy the momentum that God is building in your life, world, and affairs. Disorder causes frustration and delay, and a truly successful person knows that order creates peace, and peace is the prerequisite for *extraordinary* living. Putting your life in order keeps you in line with where God is taking you.

> *"...be sure that everything is done properly and in order"*
> I Corinthians14:40 (NLT)

Key #7: Rest.

Rest restores you and energizes you. Being rested clarifies your decision-making. An effective person never makes an important decision when tired. When you are tired, you are less open to the wise counsel of others. When you are tired, your focus will usually turn to a short-term fix rather than a long-term gain.

> *"And the God of all grace, who called you to his eternal*
> *glory in Christ, after you have suffered a little while,*
> *will himself restore you and make you strong, firm, and*
> *steadfast. To him be the power forever and ever. Amen."*
> 1 Peter 5:10–11 (NIV)

Fatigue makes you an easier target for offense. Little things that you would normally ignore will push you over the edge when you are drained. Tired people say and do things they later regret. Be aware that those are the times when you are most vulnerable, and selfishly take preventative steps to safeguard yourself.

To be effective, you must be at your best. Rest will rejuvenate you and bring things into proper perspective. Jesus knew the importance of rest. He says to His disciples,

> *"Let's get away from the crowds for a while and rest."*
> Mark 6:31 (NLT)

God sets your seasons, but your wisdom schedules them. From The Message Bible, Jesus told His disciples in John 6:12,

> *"I still have many things to tell you, but*
> *you can't handle them now."*

You see what you are prepared to see. Your present is based on your present knowledge. Your present circumstances are consistent with your present knowledge. Your "presidential authority" is tied directly to your present knowledge. John F. Kennedy said, "Leadership and learning are indispensable to each other."

As a leader, you must realize that your knowledge has exponential impact. What you communicate has far-reaching effects that cannot be underestimated. As a leader, God holds you responsible for what you know. He commands you to get with them (your group, followers, or audience) and get understanding. Proverbs 4:7 says,

> *"Wisdom is the principal thing: therefore get wisdom*
> *and with all thy getting, get understanding."*

Yet, it amazes me the number of leaders that have decided to stop learning. Too many refuse to invest in books, technological resources, and good seminars as means of education. The price of leadership is the responsibility that your personal development is seriously exemplified by never missing an opportunity to learn and grow. There is a definite reason that you were born at this time in history where knowledge is so readily available.

"To whom much is given much is required."
Luke 12:48

SECTION TWO: MEETING THE PEOPLE

Chapter 3

Guidance for People
Dr. Lee Roy Jefferson

*"A good man sheweth favour, and lendeth: he
will guide his affairs with discretion."*
Psalm 112:5

Manhood: Three Things Grown Men Need to Know

1. **Mentoring:** Mentoring is a key for men because we need a positive person, someone whose values are relatable. This has happened for me. Different people have been models and helped to shape me in terms of my values. From mentoring, comes instruction, perspective, and direction.

2. **Friendship:** Men need to find and increase their friendship with other men. We need other men with whom to talk, share, study, and enjoy positive, wholesome recreation. When things happen in our lives, we need another male to talk to—to receive instruction and gain perspective. A close circle of friends with whom we share valuable, quality time can be such a resource.

3. **The Value of Gender Differences:** Men need to recognize and appreciate gender differences—understand that they exist…then *really* "get" the conflict of the old and new nature. The issue of commitment/non-commitment still looms, as many do not know/show our duties and responsibilities as men. We simply need perspective and tools to learn how to master the role.

To grow away from dominating and controlling, we need to understand that men and women **are** different—and to understand how uniquely God has made the genders. God has made us to complement, not dominate the other. Men, sin in the world is a dominating and controlling position centered on the individual. The focus is self. Differences are valuable in the significance and success of our relationships.

The "old nature" is to dominate and control, but "the new nature" is to help, serve, and encourage. That is the Christian view of the new life in Christ…even of our life and relationship with Him. Those who have a relationship with Him are able to respect differences, by complementing and supporting the other through unity in Christ.

Young Men: Seven Recommendations for Success

1. **Be mindful of your attitude**: If you act rebellious and negative, or act as if others "owe" you, it will hinder your efforts and your road may be much harder to tow. This is true for all people. When you change your attitude, you change your life.

2. **Follow leadership**: Learn how to follow, and what is working and not working. Through your experiences, you will learn to become a leader.

3. **Respect and honor the elders**: There is something to be said for experience. While you may not always agree, wisdom is gained when you do so in respect and honor for those who came before you.

4. **Become a part of a church ministry**: This will support your growth and development. It will give you a good foundation for friendship, fellowship, goal setting, accomplishment, and victory.

5. **Help a person or a group who is in need**: Honor and service shall be cornerstones for your future. There are probably youth younger than you who would *really* appreciate knowing you.

6. **Show love to your family**: You inherited them, and they you. All deserve to receive love—especially from you.

7. **Seek to honor God in all things.**

Womanhood: Woman, the Core of the Family
3 Tips to Help Women with Your Men:

1. **Encourage your man**: Compliment him to lift him up as a unique and valuable person. Consistently show him and tell him how much he matters to you and to your family.

2. **Be there**: Motivate him to lift him in spirit by being there when you are needed in a relationship that you share, and not control. Exercise patience and insight. The power of presence in mind and spirit, not just physical presence, has meaning.

3. **Listen**: Let him know you are listening. Talk to your mate. Be "relatable," but also be a good listener. Remember, at times, that a strong woman, because of her focus in trying to convey a message and achieve solution, can sometimes lose the ability to listen when she should *really* listen and not talk. Women, it is invaluable when you can simply listen and demonstrate, "I'm here, and I'm being supportive." A man finds value in that trait.

3 Tips to Help Women Communicate with Men:

1. **Be sensitive to the tone of your voice**: Avoid a harsh, demanding, and authoritative tone in communicating with men. When a woman uses such a tone, men may be made to feel uncomfortable and threatened. They will consider the woman to be controlling. When you are sure and confident in who you are and what you desire, your tone tends to be less harsh, more acceptable, and relatable because you have nothing to prove.

2. **Dress the part**: "Anything goes" is the wrong guide. It's the wrong attitude. Be guided by the purpose and function of where you are going to determine your style of dress. Kindly avoid the wrong attire. Represent the feminine, dignified traits of women in all contexts.

3. **Seek healing**: Do not delay the process of attempting to heal when you are hurt. There is a Healer for your hurts. "Seek healing," means that, whether you or another female have experienced injury, hurt, or physical or emotional abuse, you will not accept it nor hold it in your heart without seeking healing from the hurt. An illustration is the 2009 incident

of Chris Brown and Rihanna. The incident signaled the presence of dominant and controlling personalities within their relationship, with poor results and tragic consequences of abuse. Dominant and controlling personalities can be a problem in every area of life, including the workplace where dealing with the overbearing employer's attitudes and actions toward employees can also result in tragedy.

Young Women: When Dealing with Men and Selecting a Mate

1. **Know and be yourself**: You must know who you are. "Act" who you are—respectable and a valuable, precious child of God who deserves support, encouragement, and good treatment. That sets the foundation for your relationship to another person.

2. **Have and hold to goals:** Know your goals. Be clear on them and your direction. Stay with them as you meet potential mates.

3. **Be discerning**: Practice screening. Women once screened men to see if they qualified for a sound relationship, and if they found that they were not qualified, women said "next" and moved on. Sadly, this is not true now in many instances. Screen the man you meet by asking basic questions when you meet him.

    Questions to ask:
    *   *Who are you?*
    *   *What have you done?*
    *   *Where are you headed?*

- *What have been your associations, experiences, and who has influenced them?*
- *What are you doing now?*

These questions, along with behavior that you observe, will help you to discover if he is the type of person who can complement you and help you be your best.

Once you have answers to these questions, and you have seen with your "real eyes," determine if the person is a possible asset or liability.

4. **Don't "express love" before receiving a commitment:** Every time that couples share or "express love" before a commitment, the relationship is poised for sabotage. The woman needs to receive a commitment. This practical and logical expectation is being distorted and misunderstood in today's culture, especially by young women. Just because a young man washes his car, takes a bath, dresses well, and spends $150 on a date, there should be no commitment, obligation, or responsibility on a woman's part owed to a man, because he behaved, the way a gentleman does. If the woman does the proper screening, this negative situation will probably not come up.

Keys to Long Term Marriage: Things Husbands and Wives Need to Know

"…Submitting yourselves one to another in the fear of God."
Ephesians 5:21

1. Mates should both be Christian because it is difficult for the wife to submit to the husband and the husband to provide

for the wife when the two of them have not committed to Christ. It's difficult to submit to each other when the submission to Christ has not occurred. The relationship ends up as conditional. It should be *unconditional.* It is unconditional only when both accept Christ—that is love through Christ. Marriage needs to have "love through Christ" as a spiritual foundation.

2. Mates must understand their roles. Be able to answer the questions, "What am I to do for you?" and "What do you need for me to do?" Understand the roles. Do not assume that, as mates, each knows the assumed role. Do not bring in someone as an authority who is a faulty model of a relationship—this includes people you know personally, and others. This is an affront to the partner. Mates must get to know each other for themselves. Reading newspapers and magazines and taking ideas presented there as gospel about relationships causes mates to fall victim to wrong concepts. Also, remember that the media is full of wrong or false concepts, which are simply trendy, cultural, and misleading.

3. Avoid "trendy." By doing so, you won't end up in pain— injured emotionally, spiritually, and maybe even physically.

4. Couples need a spiritual relationship with God to solidify their relationship with one another.

Chapter 4

Guidance on Family with Extraordinary Examples

*"These days should be remembered and observed
in every generation by every family, and in
every province and in every city…"*
Esther 9:28 (NIV)

Five Things You *Really* Need to Know about "Family"
Dr. Lee Roy Jefferson

1. **The Value of Family**: Your career, personal style…all of that is wonderful; yet, the core is family. When you need people to be with you, to support you, and to stand by you, it's family.

   That's what has *really* nurtured me…it is the family that has sustained me. The reason I'm in New Jersey is family. I felt that New Jersey was more conducive to the needs of my family, rather than Chicago. When Reverend Jesse Jackson asked me to become the National Director of Operation Push, it would have required me to live in Chicago, and to travel so very much. The two people who had been in the position previously had their marriages end in divorce because there was so much travel involved, as it was very demanding. The job gave no support or development to a marriage or relationship. I took a hard look at the situation and made the choice to be with my family, and it was one of the best decisions I ever made…

2. **Faith in God**: You need something to keep you focused on goals, and on priorities. Stay grounded in relation to family and what is *really* important for a good life.

I have come to a point in my life at which I have developed some principles—standards for my life—and I'm not going to allow persons or situations to move me in different directions. We all face the winds of temptations to do *something*…progress, change; but, we need an anchor to hold us to our core values rather than be enticed to do something that we'd rather not or shouldn't do.

One of the strong forces is peer pressure. Everyone wants belonging and acceptance—those are *really* strong factors. You see it in terms of group behavior and even group mentality. Many people identify strongly with groups and become a part of circles and situations that rule their lives. They "hang out with," and they "associate with" people who are weakening them. Find support through your faith, and surround yourself with others who believe and who will support your true growth and development.

3. **Get a Handle on Finances**: Understand the value of money, the use of money, and the value and importance of compound interest.

If someone had explained the *power* of it to me and the wisdom of investing, I'd be on a beach today…if only I had learned it. Most of us aren't taught the use and management of money, and most persons start out in debt and then must learn to resist credit cards, usually after the damage has been done.

Especially if you are in college, you should know that credit card companies will give the university as much as $5 million dollars to come, do credit card promotions, and then give a rebate on purchases. Credit cards cause so much trouble because we all want it "now." The banks and companies see their potential wealth based on the consumer's indebtedness. Education about finances needs to start at an early age. When people start there, it's usually for the rest of their lives that they benefit.

It's difficult to get out of debt. For example, Christmas can be one of the most devastating times of the year. The trap of debt is rooted in needs of acceptance and belonging during that season more than at any other time of the year. At Christmas, the most important thing should be getting together with loved ones. It is important for this economic era that families set a basic limit on spending.

4. **Service, the Substance of Life**: It's important that you find a cause. We've come into this world to help and serve others. As we serve others, we become the by-product of serving and helping others. When we lose ourselves for the cause of others, God blesses us. Jesus taught that what you do for others demonstrates your appreciation and love through Him—in other words, as we serve others, we are honoring God.

5. **The Value of Teaching Young Children:** Teach children so that they will be able to get the right perspective and establish the right priorities early. There are so many people or voices pulling them in different directions.

Children and teens are being led astray by principles of the world and culture. We all must help children at a young age. Push them to achieve, not just to be accepted as a part of a group or of an association. They must be taught to recognize what they should do and what they shouldn't do as they grow into adulthood—manhood and womanhood.

Growing up, I was fed by a spiritual environment in the home—*not a cultural environment.* The home and the right association in terms of being mentored are key pieces. Where people are headed is based on who reaches them or makes contact with them first—someone who is spiritual or cultural ("of the world") will reach them. Most core contacts are "friendships" through meetings, conferences, activities. People meet and begin to develop from what and with whom they make contact. It is urgent that they make the right ones.

Society, Family, Values, Beliefs, Practices, and Habits Are So Different Now...

What's the Difference?

You don't commonly find mothers as role models in motherhood. During the end of the 60's and the beginning of the 70's, things started to change. There was a stronger Spiritual Environment before then. Conservative versus Liberal, of course, is at work in the tenor of the times. Today, people have become more liberal. In the past, a more conservative era, there was a greater respect for caution and deliberation. There was also greater respect for authority—*and for those in authority*—be they teachers, ministers, parents, or elders.

Three Gifts to Young Mothers
Dr. Lee Roy Jefferson

1. **Seek a Close Relationship with God:** I believe the mother is the central role of the family in terms of influence, character, behavior, and development. That becomes more evident when you have a spiritual mother. For example, the spiritual mother demands accountability. Guided by the Word, she wants to know the whereabouts of family members and with whom they associate. She strives to protect their soul, as well as their person.

2. **Read the Word of God:** It is in the Word of God from which the mother gains strength for her life and her family as she is led by the Holy Spirit. It's through the Word that the mother gets her direction and her leadership. All of life evolves from the core of the spiritual life, which comes through the Word of God and prayer. The heart of ministry is worship, so the word of God ought to be her guide, her gauge, as she studies and meditates.

3. **Share Your Struggles with Your Children:** Because the good mother and the father feel they are the models for the family, they often withhold from their children that they are struggling financially. For example, sometimes parents buy children apparel, such as expensive sneakers or jerseys they cannot afford. However, if parents are honest with children about finances, it can be a lesson in personal strength and character building for their children.

"The next thing I knew, my legs had turned to jelly."
Dr. Edwin Bailey

A Father's Tale: Valuing the Breath of Life
Edwin Bailey, Jr., PhD

Note to Readers from Jo Lena Johnson: *I attended college at the University of Missouri-Columbia (Mizzou). While I was enrolled, I participated in the INROADS/St. Louis Summer Internship Program for four long, extraordinary summers. During that time, while we were receiving our formal educations, we were also being groomed for corporate leadership. Also during that time, I met some extremely bright and talented mentors, peers, and friends.*

One of those friends was smart, handsome, tall, hard-working, fun, good-hearted Edwin Bailey III. I liked him, I admired him and…I miss him. Because he is no longer with us, I asked his father, Dr. Bailey, if he would be willing to answer a few questions and share because I really want people to live, and to take rules, such as wearing seatbelts, seriously.

As a Communication and Leadership Trainer/Facilitator, I often assist people in learning how to focus on the five main areas of life, while managing and overcoming some of the conflicts that naturally come along with living. These areas of life include Health, Relationships/Family, Education/Career, Finance, and Community/Spirituality. I show people how to focus on the things they really want versus things they don't. Later in the book, I'll go into more detail about this; however, because we really want you to live extraordinarily, this is a great time to introduce you to Dr. Bailey.

In sharing his very personal story and wisdom, Dr. Bailey covered the five main areas of life so well and even emphasized Dr. Jefferson's Key #7— Rest. Thus, we decided to devote this section to one of his personal stories. As you begin reading, I want you to know Dr. Bailey's two favorite songs are "I Won't Complain" and "I've Got a Testimony."

It was a blessing to me to listen to him—may it be a blessing to you to read it. In the beginning of our conversation, he was so chipper that I asked him how he could sound so lively so early in the morning (it was about 7:30 am). He explained that he was a morning person and then began sharing his routine with me. When he began speaking of his health habits, I started typing what he had to share. To really live, it's so important to pay attention to even the "little things." While some of the "story" may be sad, I ask you to learn from it, and to care for your family and yourself in healthy, responsible ways. After all, we are all connected.

Dr. Bailey Shares:

> *Edwin Franklin Bailey, III—"Teddy" Is the name*
> *I gave him when he was born, July 8, 1970.*

My Daily Personal Care Routine: Great for…
Those Eligible for AARP!

One Glass of Organic Apple Cider Vinegar with 6–7 glasses of water. I eat an apple and a banana with high fiber cereal along with a bicycling or boxing workout 30 minutes per day for five days a week, along with stretching. I do all of this by 7 am because I'm a morning person. Then I read my Bible, and that is usually done by 7:30. A few years ago, I noticed that I had gained weight and didn't like the results, given that I was close to 60 years old at the time. I realized that in order to lose weight and to lose it permanently, I was going to have to exercise, be disciplined, and eliminate fast food—not completely—the key is to make sure I am not eating it on a regular basis and it doesn't become part of my regular pattern. I avoid juices on the shelf because they have little nutritional value and are so high in calories and sugar—I cut out juices, most soda, and I use olive oil for cooking and sautéing.

If people would cut down eating fast food by even 50%, it would help with losing weight and maintaining weight loss. I am from St. Louis, so every now and then I get the "White Castle call." I just order a few of the burgers without cheese, and then don't eat them again for 2 or 3 months. It's not that you can't eat fast food, just don't do it on a regular basis.

There is another "hometown" place I enjoy—Lamar's Donut Shop. I go there twice a year, and I will get 3 or 4 of my favorite donuts— that works for me. If I did that every day, I would put on weight. So now, it's just a part of becoming aware of food, food groups, and educating yourself and about the things you eat that can affect your body…I have lost 30 pounds gradually over the last 3 years. According-ing to the BMI chart, I still have 7 pounds to go. I'm doing it so it's not drastic and is worked into my daily lifestyle. It's possible, with discipline, to achieve your goals without giving up everything you like completely.

My friend Edwin passed on Saturday, Sept 24, 1994 at about 7:24 am, after falling asleep at the wheel. ~ Jo Lena Johnson

Spirit Lead Me to Call My Son that Evening…

The Friday before my son "Teddy" died…I was Dean of Students at the Meramec Campus of the St. Louis Community College…I was at my desk, and spirit lead me to call and touch base with him. I was surprised that he answered the phone…we had the longest telephone conversation we had ever had. We talked about everything a father and son could talk about—his girlfriend, his friends, his love life, his finances, just everything you would want to talk about.

His mother, Gwendolyn Weddington Bailey, had just died five months earlier on April 19, 1994, and I had put him in touch with a financial advisor to assist him with his inheritance. We were talking about that process and how he had been advised. We then talked about health, eating the right foods, exercise, movies, and his job. Finally, he ended the conversation by telling me that he and his friend Charles Wilson were going to a wedding reception later that evening.

That Saturday morning around 11 o'clock, I was at home getting ready to fix some pizza and had the storm door open. A man walked on to my porch wearing a sports coat, and there was something about his demeanor and his walk that let me know he was a police officer—I don't know how I knew. I opened the door, and he asked me if I was Edwin Bailey, Jr. I said yes. He identified himself as a Hazelwood Detective and informed me that my son had been in an automobile accident. Initially, I thought he was talking about my teenage son who had been out the night before and who was upstairs asleep. I asked, "What did he do, sideswipe a car?" He said, "No, I'm not talking about Louis, the youngest, I'm talking about Edwin."

Then I said, "Well, what about him?" He said, "There was an automobile accident early this morning, and he did not survive." And when he said those words, the next thing I knew my legs had turned to jelly. I was on the floor; I literally lost it. And that was probably the most traumatic thing I've ever experienced in my life. For the next several days, I was in a daze. My daughter Ericka had to come home for the second time in five months to bury someone dear to her. I can only imagine what she too went through.

Without Proper Rest, People Can Lose Focus and More…

Apparently, after the reception they stopped at a couple of clubs on the East Side (East St. Louis, IL) and were out all night. When the accident occurred, they were headed back to Florissant. From an eye-witness report, I learned he had fallen asleep at the wheel. Both had fallen asleep, when the road began to curve and the car began to roll into the gravel. Apparently, he woke up and tried to straighten out the car. The car became airborne, flipped over the embankment, and rolled over 2 or 3 times—I know this part because I talked to Charles and asked him to tell me what had happened.

He said that when he woke up, the car was airborne, that it flipped, and finally rested upside down. Edwin didn't have his seatbelt on. He had a massive head injury. Thankfully, he expired from the head injuries moments after the accident and never regained consciousness, which our family views as a blessing from God. He was 24 years old when he died. He had just had a birthday and died on the 24th of the month of September. Charles, thank God, had walked away with only a slight head injury.

We began planning Teddy's funeral service. It was very difficult. During that time, it seemed so surreal. I lay down to take naps, and I would awake to think that maybe I just had a bad dream. However, I was dealing with reality. At the visitation, the line at Wade Funeral Home stretched out to the parking lot…because so many had known him, and had gone to high school and college with him. Their tributes were so uplifting.

Questions Asked of Dr. Bailey:
What three things do you really want to say Young People?

1. Value everyday and make sure you express your love and caring to people around you.

2. Understand your limitations and never push yourself physically beyond those limitations. My son had worked that day; he went to a wedding reception and literally stayed up all night; and, he literally fell asleep trying to make it home. Make sure you get enough rest, physically.

3. Never drive when you are exceptionally drowsy or under the influence of alcohol. And, always wear your seat belt. Had Edwin been wearing his, he may well have survived the accident because the injury he sustained was from his head hitting the roof of the vehicle. And, I believe that's what saved Charles. He was wearing his seatbelt.

What are Parental Responsibilities to a Son?

1. To serve as a positive model for him from Manhood, Spirituality, being financially secure and stable to teaching him to take care of his own needs and possibly a family in the future. It was my responsibility to prepare my son for the future.

2. To provide appropriate advice and guidance to him, to assist him in his development and maturity.

3. To ensure that he values the concept of family, and to instill within him strong family values.
   - To show, to be available to, and to love and care for family members—including extended family.
   - To help him recognize he represents his family in terms of what one does outside of the household, in the community, and in the work place.
   - To help him understand the Sanctity and the power of the family model—that is husband, wife, children, parents, etc.
   - To link family to a spiritual concept: the family ought to be held in high regard, to link back to Adam and Eve in Genesis when God put them together and gave them the ability to procreate and have children. The concept of family flows back to the Bible, just like that first family, with a spiritual connection.

4. To hold aloft the value of education and hard work—for my children, not just my son. They both worked hard.

What are Additional Parental Responsibilities to a Daughter?

1. To make sure she is safe and protected. Even as an adult, my daughter will always be my baby girl.

2. To make sure that she knows that she is loved and will always have a place of honor within the family.

3. To always try to inspire her to be the most prolific woman she can be—and these three are in addition to the things from the "son" list, of course.

What do you to Really want to say to Parents?

1. Make sure that your children know they are loved and held in high esteem.

2. Give your children as much quality time as you can—time wherein the *children are the focus of your attention.*

3. You need to make sure that your children receive appropriate religious education and values, to insure that children are provided every opportunity to grow and develop in as many ways as possible through the gifts and talents that God has provided them.

Why do you conduct a Prison Ministry?

It is a calling that I have from God to spread the Gospel for Jesus Christ and to provide spiritual encouragement to those, who in many cases, have been "written off by our society."

1. Statistics, plus history and practice, have shown that many prisoners will be returned to society. It is important for them to come back with a renewed sense of purpose and to be able to cope successfully with a sometimes hostile and unwelcoming environment.

2. It's important to make sure that individuals who don't have ready access to God's word are given an opportunity to attend services and to be exposed to information of a Spiritual nature that perhaps they would not have access to otherwise.

3. Prisoners tell us that they derive a great deal of satisfaction from the ministry and that it is encouraging to know that there are people who have not written them off and are willing to take their personal time to come and share with them. Most importantly, they can potentially get the opportunity to be Saved.

Richard Lovelace, who lived in the 1600's, wrote the poetic lines, "Stone walls do not a prison make, nor iron walls a cage," and I agree with that assessment. And, while Baptism is not a requirement for salvation (as Jesus already died so that we might be saved), it is an open proclamation (it shows) that one has had an inward change from the heart. It *should* be an open proclamation. This is a sign, a symbol that one has undergone a regenerated heart and is walking in the newness of life through Jesus Christ.

"Aren't you glad I talked too much?"
Alice Grey, at 8 years old

A Mother's Pride and Love: Sacrifices and Blessings
Wisdom from Alice Grey

Alice Grey is the mother of two daughters. She believes that education is extremely important and chose to live in one room so that she could pay for her daughters to get through college. She didn't want them be distracted or taken off course by anything that would prevent them from achieving their goals. She made a promise to them: "If you go to college, I will work to pay for your education through your Bachelor's Degree." So far, the investment has paid off!

She has been so committed to keeping her promise that she is willing to do all that is in her power to assist her children in living better lives. College preparation for their family includes:

- Relationship Building: Providing babysitting services for her grandchildren *(quality time with grandma);*

- Books: Providing the tools necessary and required for instruction and learning;

- Rent: Providing a stable home in which to live, study, and feel safe and secure as family;

- Clothing: Providing a necessary element of life that is sometimes not considered in planning a budget; and

- Tuition: Providing the cost of the classes and associated fees.

While reading about Alice Grey, you may be thinking, "So what?" "What's the big deal?"

Well, the big deal is that Alice Grey is not a materially rich woman with the luxury of a trust fund, inheritance or other wealth. Alice works every day at Prince George's Community College in Largo, Maryland. She gives and gives with her infectious smile and outgoing personality. She seems not to meet strangers and welcomes each with a kind word, a good tip, or by answering the question to address the need, which brings people into her office.

When asked why providing resources is so important to her, she tells a little story about her childhood.

"My parents divorced when I was about 7 or 8 years old...I remember a while after that happened—when we literally ran out of food. My mother took one can of beans, and made hot water corn bread, and we split it between all of us children. It was not enough food to eat, so she did not eat."

For one week, we couldn't go to school because my mom said we didn't have any food—she was afraid that, because I talked too much, I would tell others about our situation. One day my teacher called my mom, but she wasn't home. When the teacher asked me why none of us had been at school, I said, "How are we going to go to school if we don't have food to eat?"

My teacher said, "Tell your mom to call me when she gets home." I gave my mom the message. Yet, I didn't say anything about what I had told her about being hungry and not having enough to eat. The next day, we had two red wagons full of food! And I said to my mom, "Aren't you glad I talked too much?"

Alice worked at the Ford Motors plant for 20 years in order to put her children through school. Daily she wore a skirt, heels, and stockings to the factory. She says, "I didn't want my kids to aspire to work in a factory, so I had to show them something different." Although working in a factory, she took the attitude, "This is my office. I'm 'keeping hope alive' until my oldest daughter gets out of high school." She told everyone that she was going to retire when she reached that mark. At age 40, she did, in fact, retire and leave Detroit.

A friend helped Alice get a job at Prince George's Community College where she has worked since leaving Detroit. Back then, she was using a typewriter, and later moved to an area with a "TV on the desk" and didn't know what to do with it. That "TV" was a personal computer. She took initiative—practiced, studied, learned how to use it. Alice says, "I sat at the computer sun up to sun down teaching myself." It paid off because Alice excelled to such proficiency that she now teaches software to others.

When you *really* want something, few things, if any, can keep you from achieving your goals.

"Getting into Mom Mode"
Wisdom Simply Spoken
Daryle Glynn Brown

Ms. Brown shares:

1. Be calm and assuring—even if you are not calm and assured!

2. Give lots of hugs!

3. Offer advice in a manner that might be readily accepted.

4. Do research so you are well versed and know as much as possible about the subject, topic, or challenge.

5. Offer to go to doctor's appointments (or others)—offer a listening ear because sometimes you might hear something they don't—and to be there for support.

Yes, be you a mom, a dad, or simply a good friend, everyone has gotten into "Mom Mode" when it counts. And, if this is our own "human" idea—imagine Our Father's idea and mode for us!

> *"Now to Him who is able to do exceedingly abundantly above all that we ask or think, according to the power that works in us, to Him be glory…"*
> Ephesians 3:20–21 (NKJV)

Chapter 5

Guidance on Education with Extraordinary Examples

> *"You are our letter, written in our hearts, known and read by all men; being manifested that you are a letter of Christ, cared for by us, written not with ink but with the Spirit of the living God, not on tablets of stone but on tablets of human hearts."*
> 2 Corinthians 3:2–3 (New American Standard)

Dr. Jefferson's Message to Youth: "The University of Adversity"

Introductory Note from Dr. Jefferson: *The following excerpt is from a Sermon given at Concord Baptist Church on Sunday, June 23, 1991. I gave it on the "coming of age" of my daughter Erica, as she reached her 16th birthday. She had been granted a summer scholarship to study chemistry and mathematics at William Paterson College in Wayne, New Jersey, and I was moved to share some things from my heart and head, as a father and as a Minister. I share it in this book because, just as that day when I was speaking to my own child, I want each young person who reads this book, or is affected by this book, to be prepared to live a better life in Christ. So I say...*

Please understand that, because you are an open letter, you will face some adversity.

Notre Dame is a great Catholic University. Oxford is a great English University. Columbia is a great New York University.

The "University of Adversity" is a "suffering university." Jesus told us that "in this life we would have trials and tribulations…" that's why the University of Adversity has a long and distinguished honor roll of graduates…in suffering, disappointment, and let down. I wish I could protect you from life's adversities, but I cannot. G. A. Young states that some face adversity through the waters; some through the fire; some through great sorrow;…but all through the blood. None of us can escape difficulty. That's why all of us will face some adversity.

You must continue to resist peer pressure.

I know that in your world growing up is different from the world in which I grew up. When I was growing up, my community had clear values, clear standards, and clear convictions. You live in a world of violence, racism, AIDS, rebellion, extreme individualism, disrespect, deception, corruption, drugs, and too much exposure to things that are negative. I know that life in the world in which you live is not easy. That is why you must continue to resist peer pressure. You must not be guided by your peers. You must stand for something. You must continue to make your parents, your church, and your God proud of you. You must resist peer pressure…

1. So that you can reach your goals;

2. So that you can become successful;

3. So that you can avoid being misled.

You must watch the company you keep.

There is truth in the old saying "Birds of a feather flock together." Blessings favor those who watch the company they keep. Blessings favor those who are home before midnight. Nothing good happens after midnight.

Finally, you must continue an abiding faith in God.

Your mother and I are grateful that you have declared publicly your faith in God. As you go to William Paterson College, continue an abiding faith in God. I do not mean that you should walk around waving a banner, but let your faith be the evidence in all that you do. You live in a troubled world. Be not weary in well doing, for in due season you shall reap if you faint not. George Bernard Shaw said, "Some people see things and say why? But, others see things that never were and say why not?"

And I know, if I'll only be true to this glorious quest, that my
heart will lie peaceful and calm, when I'm laid to my rest.
And the world will be better for this; that one man,
Scorned and covered with scars,
still strove with his last ounce of courage
to reach the unreachable stars.
To dream the impossible dream to fight the unbeatable foe,
To bear with unbearable sorrow, to run where the brave dare not go.
To right the unrightable wrong, to love pure and chaste from afar,
To try when your arms are too weary, to reach the unreachable star!
This is my quest, to follow that star, no matter how hopeless,
No matter how far; to fight for the right without question or pause.
To be willing to march into hell for a heavenly cause!
Lyrics written by Joe Darion

∞

"The stakes are high…"
Dr. Lee Roy Jefferson

"Thrusting, Bragging, and Such Are Just Nonsense"
Vera Raglin

Vera Raglin, Veteran Educator, Writes Her Message to Teachers and Parents:

Note to Readers from Jo Lena: *Vera Raglin was my 11th Grade Honors English Teacher at Riverview Gardens High School in (North County) St. Louis, Missouri. She's a veteran educator, a mother, and a wise woman who has been extremely influential in my life. I really want people to learn from her, and I am honored that she was willing to participate in this book series by submitting this piece, and by her tremendous efforts to coach me through the writing process.*

Whether you are a student, parent, teacher, church leader, business owner, or simply a concerned citizen, Mrs. Raglin demonstrates honor, commitment, leadership, integrity, love of teaching and learning. A few pages of her wisdom are worth their weight in gold!

Six Things I *Really* Want Teachers to Know

1. As a teacher, you are always a learner.

2. You can't teach kids you don't take opportunity to know—and for whom you don't allow opportunity to know you.

3. Because people and actions are always connected, there is no way for you to mistreat a child and not have it come back to you.

4. Students should be prepared to take care of the world one day, just as you and I as children were taught to do our part in taking care of the world. Teaching should be a revered position. It's not to be taken lightly when you are training a mind for optimal results in knowing, being, and doing.

5. Students have the right to learn how to think. If you don't teach them how to think, they won't know how to live. Thinking is what is going to save them—and all of us. It's not always all about teaching subject matter at the start. What is ultimately important for your students is that they master the ability to process information: to know through understanding. Once exposed to information, knowledge comes as a result of analyzing, synthesizing, and never failing to evaluate what one hears, sees, and even thinks. Students can't learn how to think by simply memorizing someone else's ideas. If you teach them how to think and imagine, they will be able to choose what information will be useful for their own future…livelihood, well-being, career, citizenship, humanity. Students need to have a point of reference in the things taught and required to learn, to be able to relate those things to something they already know, care about—have already "studied"—or can use. What they read and learn— and the *way* it is presented—should be something that will forever help students make good decisions. And, believe me; *that is your grave responsibility.*

6. Low self-esteem leads to rebellion. There is probably nothing worse in school for a child than sitting in a room where

everyone else knows "stuff" he/she doesn't know. When children don't know such things as decorum and are doubly embarrassed by not having academic skills, it makes them unable to think logically in the moment. Yes, they act out in the classroom, but they will act out even more so in life without mastery of big and little things. You are creating a monster when you don't teach a child. There is joy for children in learning, and there is a joy for real teachers in watching children learn—watching them become able to understand and explore…observe someone else's creativity and, in doing so, gain access to their own. To teach is to help a child discover self, personal talents, goals—along with connections to others and the use of the gift of life only for good."

Ms. Raglin…Just Thinking…

"When the "Standards" came into instruction, I thought, as an educator, it would be the one way we could ensure that all students would get the same quality education (although funding would be screwed up). As a child coming up through segregated schools, I was a part of a generation of students who were forced to study from ten or fifteen year old books—the books slowly drifting in from the white schools after their students got new books. Still, we learned what was presented because our teachers went the extra mile. We were able to do experiments in chemistry and biology with no modern science books, no modern equipment only because teachers knew their content; and, they knew and cared about their students. Their personal time and money was spent in finding equipment and other resources. They even taught us things we didn't learn at home. Told us and illustrated for us how to be well groomed, to be respectful, and to have high self-esteem. They taught us the basics and then went on to teach us the curriculum, which was clear cut and focused."

"It's wonderful when a teacher is "called to teach"—because not only is it necessary to know the science of teaching, it is ideal to understand the *art* of teaching. My teachers in my segregated, supposedly, disadvantaged schools found many ways to introduce what students needed to know. They proved that teachers are able to produce, to teach when it is in the head and heart. Truly, if it's not there, students don't—won't learn. They won't make it. I can't imagine being a little kid in a situation where nobody really likes me—a school where nobody really cares, where they watch me everyday flounder and yet throw out no lifeline. It must be awful…it is."

"Now and ever, private schools will flourish as long as people don't like what's happening in most public schools. Coming into existence, there will be more and more charter and magnet schools as public schools, but with limited spaces. Some people will run to these. Of course, then there will be more and more slum schools; but many parents and their children won't run from these, for one reason or another. However, they might be forced to run or forced to remain trapped there. Where will they have left to go…virtual schools? Access to those schools will get to be very expensive, but people who have money can always educate their kids. Most African-Americans, of course, along with the *poor or other poor*—will probably be at the bottom…still."

"Recently, African American students on the elementary level have been improving and closing the gap in many instances, but the gains are not occurring on the secondary level, especially in low income metropolitan areas. Yet, among urban schools where focus is drastically needed, there are those that don't have a written curriculum or wherein teachers don't follow the curriculum—which means that teachers are teaching what they like, what's easiest for teachers, or nothing of substance at all. And, of course, many parents—overwhelmed or uninformed—don't make demands of their children or the schools for improvement. This has to change."

"Education is at the root of most things we do now and at the root of most things that we will be able to do in the future. Knowledge allows us to have wisdom, and it also guides our thinking...which includes knowing "how to do," and "how to live," and how to save ourselves."

Questions Asked of Mrs. Raglin:
What's Missing in Education (Schools) Today?

1. Appreciation for learning;

2. The understanding that learning allows progress for humanity;

3. Realizing that learning protects our history— including personal, national, and cultural;

4. The belief that knowledge is sacred;

5. Too few real teachers and real students—someone who never stops learning and who is always willing to teach. As a culture and a nation, we don't view education as a treasure and deserving of respect above materialism.

If I Could, I Would Give to Today's Teachers:

1. Love of Children;

2. Love of Ideas;

3. Love of the mission;

4. Willingness to adapt methods and strategies to contexts through flexibility, continuous honing of skills and clarity for the child who needs it and the situation that demands it;

5. Understanding that teachers should work on their teaching as an *art*, not always as a science.

What should parents know?

Parents, to Raise Well-Rounded Children, Teach Them about:

1. Independence—knowing how and when to resist conformity;

2. Opportunity to refine personal talents and skills;

3. Belief in something Spiritual—Faith, God, the Holy Spirit—something greater than self.

4. Understanding their rightful place in the universe. They need to know that they are here for a reason. Tell them: Of all of the thousands of eggs and chance events, meetings, partnerships between people, and "marriages" of people as parents, it could have been anybody as the result—but it was *you*. You are unique, and you are here for a purpose.

If children know and understand these things, chances are all the other positive things will happen…if they know what's above…know "I can't do anything without God, without others, and without *me*."

Parents, You Are Truly Your "Child's "First Teachers."

1. Make sure your children know that they are loved unconditionally.

2. Always make it clear to your children that you are preparing them for life every day and right now, so that they can always see beyond the "right now."

3. Give them experiences so they are able to make good choices. The more experiences they have, the more they understand what impacts their world. Exposure leads to their thinking and making comparisons about who they are, where they are, and what they want to be so that they can make sound choices for their future.

4. Introduce your children to hobbies and interests apart from television, radio, clothing, cars, and pointless or excessive fun. Young people are besieged by music tracks and videos. There was a time when music had meaning—worthwhile expressions of feelings for people and passion for ideas. It was even about social protest. Often, just a few decades ago, music appealed to the strengths and ideals of people. However, a lot of pop and rock music today appeals to the baseness in human beings. There is too much focus on basic instincts, even depravity. For just a few young audiences, it's *not* entertainment. Today's music advertises personality over talent. It used to be about intelligence, creativity, sensitivity, *and* talent. There were so many metaphors used to deliver meaning. Thrusting, bragging and such are just nonsense— it doesn't mean anything. Some may recall the song "If I had a Hammer" and the line, "I'd hammer out justice and love…" Those ideals support humanity. There's nothing

selfish about that—it's very giving. It's not just about "you," or your own "kind," or your self-indulgence.

Hobbies and interests are character building and relaxing. They allow the person to be introspective, especially if it's something the individual can do alone. As children enjoy hobbies, they—like anyone else—have a chance to think, to renew confidence and self-esteem, and to gain perspective.

5.   Teach your children the meaning and value of hard work. People who believe they have to deliver hard work do so because they learned to have a conscience. They believe that discipline and doing things right not only makes the world go right, but it also helps their own life go right. If you learn through family heritage, through sound traditions, through being connected outside of yourself, and through faith in the spiritual world, you have great chances for a good life. Expectations and honor to family and God keep us grounded. It's not that people who live and believe this way won't have difficulty or that, for them, life won't sometimes be hard; but, they have a *whole* set of tools. When things are hard, they won't give up. They will think and problem solve.

When I consider my own actions as I face a problem, I know I might rest, but I will always try one more thing—to find a solution or overcome obstacles. *I will not quit!*

6.   Teach children the *power of good.* A person is supposed to pass good things on. Tell children, when something kind is done for them, they should do what is kind for someone else; pass it on. Show thankfulness by doing right because right makes the world go better.

Christianity is not about just heaven or hell in the future—we can all have both, here and now in the physical world. God didn't suffer His Son to come, live, and die in so much turmoil just to demonstrate that there is a heaven for us to go to rest forever. I believe He did it to show us how we can serve here on earth. Even little things like "please," "thank you," "excuse me," or obeying traffic signals honor and respect the other person and what is right to do. Order and humility are necessary. They too are right "to do." If you are given a talent, as a teacher or for any path in life, you shouldn't hide it under the bush. Be excellent! As my father (Joseph Radford) always said, *"You don't have to be good at everything, but strive to be best at what you're good at."* Use your talent to contribute to order and right in the universe. Constantly help others grow, see ideas, and aspire to the ideal. Help others sharpen their talents so that they too can discover "what they are good at."

Remember, there is no such thing as an innocent bystander in life. Nobody should just be "standing by" in the context of living purposefully. It's not enough to try and dodge life's dangers and hardships, simply living to store up treasures on the earth for you and yours. It is not even enough if you simply warn and editorialize about the dangers and wrongs in the world. What we all must do is daily demonstrate *right* and *good* by taking a stand on the things that matter for the best of humanity through our thoughts, words, and deeds.

Pledge now to be a model of good in action. Live absolutely as a servant to this cause.

"Praying About Stuff First Makes a Difference"
Chris Bynote

Education, Choices, and Military Service: Wisdom from Chris Bynote, A Single Young Christian Man

Chris Bynote Shares:

"I was born in Kansas City in August of 1978. I grew up in Houston, and attended high school in Memphis, graduating in 1997. My mother is Gwen Randle, and my sister is Regina (Bynote) Jones, who is 7 years older than me. I'm currently attending Houston Community College, working on an Associate Degree in International Business. At work, I'm a "Field Service Technician," which means, I'm an oil rig mechanic."

Questions Asked of Chris Bynote:
What did you do upon graduation from high school?

"I went directly to the Navy."

Why?

"My dad was in the Navy, and I was attracted to the discipline, respect, and honor that being in the military brought. I also wanted to get away from the house. I felt I had a better chance of having a positive outcome in the military than at college, and it worked out that way. Being in the Navy was more challenging than the party life I could have had, at the time, in college."

In what sense was it more challenging?

"My training in the Navy was in advanced electronics, and I served for five years. It would have been easier to go to college because the military was more uncertain. It was not always easy studying, training, and making money at the same time. Yet, I knew that the discipline was better for me than my staying in Memphis, getting a job, and going to school."

What are five things you gained through your military experience?

"I learned:

1.   A good sense of organization;

2.   Leadership skills;

3.   People skills;

4.   An understanding of how the world works, especially the way people relate to one another internationally; and…

5.   Responsibility."

What is your definition of Leadership?

"Being an example. Living the right way—not giving up when you fail. A true leader doesn't have to say anything or talk a good game, he, or she, just leads by example."

How did you come to that conclusion?

"Because I realized that *a big part of life is failure, and a very, very small part of life is success.* Most of the people who are really, really successful usually failed a lot; but they just kept and do keep going. Though there are people who do live a good life, those who experience success on a higher level, who really making a big difference, those people usually have failed a lot."

Why is training important?

"Training to me, prepares you for your future. For example, Warren Buffett has planned to not leave his family any money. He knows that failure is the only way to succeed. If you give someone success, they won't pass success along. Sometimes it'll stop with them, for the most part. As another example, if I am successful in finance and give my son a million dollars, he won't be successful in finance, necessarily. But he may be successful in some other area." *(Chris has no children at this time.)*

"However, if you give someone understanding, then they can become successful. You can't succeed if you don't know yourself, know what you are good at and what you aren't. It's about learning self."

What are the effects of lack of training in the workforce?

"America needs poor people in order to function. It's the 10% who succeed; but the 90% don't stop the system, since they are people who go out and work in factories or other everyday low to middle-income jobs. It helps to have some good people who succeed with the most common income and in the most common workforce areas of life. Their actions can help or inspire someone else. They make a better world. That is not to say that someone among the 10% cannot work, relate, or inspire people for the sake of building a better world, but an individual who hurts self and others by doing less than his/her best and by stooping to the lowest levels of life is deemed "replaceable." The usual idea is that there is *always* someone who can replace you; no one is irreplaceable, especially if you are thought of as being among the masses. If people fail to get education, training, or work to develop means to live, they end up stooping to anything to live. For the person who stoops, there is jail, poverty, guns, robbing, worse crimes, and all other things that shadow life into loss. For the 10% and the 90% alike, that means loss of human potential, public safety, and the shrinking means to support us all in moving ever upward. Ultimately, the loss affects everyone."

How did you end up moving back to Houston?

"I was in Memphis, TN, in Real Estate and was renting out houses. I wasn't making the type of money I wanted to make. So I moved to Houston, where my sister lived, and where I could make a good living working in the oil fields. It has all worked out."

Why are you single?

"I choose to be single now because:

1. I'm not financially where I want to be;

2. I don't think a person should get married until they are "together" themselves;

3. I want to be able to support a house, home, and a family— and have time to devote to them and those efforts;

4. I'm just starting to get to the point where I do want to get married;

5. I'm trying to avoid going through the divorce stuff, by any means necessary."

You mentioned God earlier... What role does your faith play in your life, behavior, and habits?

- "Faith plays a big role—if not the biggest."

- "I try to pray before I make decisions. I've made a lot of decisions based on faith versus the reality of the situation. It has completely changed my life a hundred times over. For example, real estate was one of the biggest decisions for me. What I always try to do is to take good advice, even if it's not something I want to hear. I once had two duplexes and one house. I was making probably $750 per month from the rental properties, but the monthly headaches were probably worth $2,000 a month. Then, the renters stopped paying rent. I almost let them go into foreclosure. However, people advised me not to do that. I went ahead, and put them on the market. Now even seven years later, I still owe a little on them but I'll be debt free this year. Even though there's God, some things still take time. He provided me the opportunity to make money; I don't have the burden of the houses; and, it has worked out. That's one big thing. Prayer."

- "I was going to leave the job I have now for another company, and that wouldn't have been good. For the company I'm with now, I'm under contract. Prayer."

- "Praying about stuff first makes a difference; it all works out."

SECTION THREE: SHINING BRIGHTLY AND EVERYDAY LIVING

Chapter 6

Seven Ways to Show Your Brilliance with Prayer and Affirmations
Jo Lena Johnson

"Arise, shine; for thy light is come, and the glory of the Lord is risen upon thee."
Isaiah 60:1

Showing Your Brilliance

Not long ago, I wrote a book called <u>A Light is Born.</u> It is a "baby book" intended to instill character, positive thinking, sensitivity, and good habits from the beginning, when the child is born. Studies show that most human beings establish self-concept and basic thoughts about themselves and others between the ages of two and seven years old. I want adults to have easy ways to help encourage and "grow" their children's minds and experiences early and extraordinarily.

Psalm 46:8–10 from The Message Bible reads,

"Attention, all! See the marvels of GOD*! He plants flowers and trees all over the earth, Bans war from pole to pole, breaks all the weapons across his knee. "Step out of the traffic! Take a long, loving look at me, your High God, above politics, above everything."*

I have chosen to share the "list" below from <u>A Light is Born</u> because I always hoped that, as parents/adults were reading to the young, they too, would begin to apply the concepts to their matured lives. I did not change the words. If as adults, we are willing to look at the basics and review what we are doing well, not doing at all, and what we must remember to do, we can begin to live in a manner, which cultivates life as it is meant to be.

If you are willing to live up to your own brilliance, you'll be amazed at how much extraordinary living you'll create for yourself and for others!

#1 Love!

Start now by saying, "I love me" because when you love yourself, you believe in yourself, and you know that you are lovable no matter what. Also, loving yourself teaches you how to love others as well.

In Isaiah 6:8 we read, *"Also I heard the voice of the Lord, saying, Whom shall I send, and who will go for us? Then said I, Here am I; send me."*

Imagine feeling lovable enough to "be sent by God" to demonstrate His mighty works!

When most of us grew up, we were taught to say "I love you" and to respond to "I love you." If you understand how much "you" matter, you will have the experience and wisdom to live extraordinarily in the face of life's challenges.

Affirmation:
"Abba, Father! When I miss Your mark, please
cleanse my heart, mind, and soul,
as You guide me to love. Fill me and make
me available to Your Holy Spirit.
In Jesus name, Thank You God!"

#2 Be Patient and Kind!

When there are misunderstandings, don't give up; learn to listen, to share your thoughts and feelings in ways that allow others to share with you. This will help you learn, grow; and you will become thoughtful and generous.

Proverbs 22:4 reads, *"By humility and the fear of the Lord are riches, and honour, and life."*

Fear can also mean "obedience, guidance, reverence, and listening." When we allow the Spirit of God to flow through our thoughts and feelings regularly, daily, and in times of stress, we are able to "show" patience and kindness because those are characteristics of Him.

"And Joshua said unto the people, Sanctify yourselves:
for tomorrow the LORD will do wonders among you."
Joshua 3:5

Affirmation:
"I am a Gentle Servant in Progress."

This is one my favorite personal affirmations…I try hard to live "up to it" in my behavior and attitude. Since I'm not perfect (even though I want to be), it is now a part of my life-long mantra. In service, we must be "gentle," loving and kind. Although I have a great capacity to love, I don't always "show" it mainly because I have a tendency to get impatient when things take a long time or I feel someone is less than loving. Learning "how to love others as well" can be challenging, if we are trying to rely on our "little" selves. When you sincerely claim a thing, such as a principle, and you attach your identity to it, you live it. In this light, the thing, the principle, the affirmation becomes "true" for you.

"I am" is what I mean by "attaching your identity." Who do you say you are? *I am…*

#3 Respect Yourself and Others!

Be considerate in your deeds and actions in ways that would meet the approval of your God and family at all times.

I Kings 3:5 says, *"In Gibeon the Lord appeared to Solomon in a dream by night: and God said, Ask what I shall give thee."*

King Solomon spoke to God, and he asked for something that pleased the Lord…Wisdom!

> *"Give therefore thy servant an understanding (hearing) heart to*
> *judge thy people that I may discern between good and bad…"*
> I Kings 3:9

Especially in tough times, it becomes difficult to "hold your graceful-
ness." Being grounded in your Spiritual self can make it easier to be
mindful of your best thoughts, feelings, actions, attitudes, and what
you show to others!

In tough times, affirming this slightly modified version of Psalm
25:20–22 may be of help:

Affirmation:
*"O keep my soul, and deliver me: let me not be ashamed; for I
put my trust in You. Let integrity and uprightness preserve me;
for I trust in you. Deliver me O God, out of all my troubles."*

#4 Show Good Character!

Your Spirit is good and so is your nature. You get to make good
choices so that as you grow you will be enthusiastic, positive, and
productive.

Psalm 125:4 says, *"Do good, O Lord, unto those that be good, and to
them that are upright in their hearts."*

Sometimes it's great to create an affirmation or prayer, but there are
so many that exist already! Below, you will find the words of David,
from Psalm 143:10.

Affirmation/Prayer:
*"Teach me to do your will, for you are my God; may
your good Spirit lead me on level ground."*

#5 Be a Willing Student!

Focus on completing formal education and life lessons. Learn to discover and explore new things by asking questions when you don't understand. Because, when you are willing, you become informed and wise.

Proverbs 22:12 states, *"Apply thine heart unto instruction, and thine ears to the words of knowledge."*

This is not only true for children; it's also true for everyone. As each is willing to continue learning no matter how great or small previous accomplishments, extraordinary living takes place.

Dr. Jefferson advised us to "Think Big"—as you stretch your mind with the Word of God, filled with the Spirit of God, your capacity and works will be stretched by the Presence of God.

"I delight to do thy will, O my God: yea
the law is within my heart."
Psalm 49:8

My prayer—
"I am willing. Please show me how to think big and be
clear in your sight oh, Lord God. Thanks for exposing
me to new, good ideas, that I might grow and connect
with the extraordinary You, in Jesus Name, Amen."

#6 Practice Personal Care!

This means wash your hands, clean your face, brush your teeth, comb your hair, and dress with care; have regular checkups with dentists and doctors; eat healthy food; and get exercise too.

1 Corinthians 6:19: *"Do you not know that your body is a temple of the Holy Spirit, who is in you, whom you have received from God? You are not your own."*

When you dress, practice hygiene, choose certain foods, fail to exercise, or rest, do you consider others in your life that are affected by what you do and don't do? Epidemics and illnesses that cripple and shorten life happen many times because people don't love themselves. Learn to appreciate you.

Some things are just unacceptable!

When you see young people who may or may not be related to you, what do you think about their attire or habits? What do you think that those same young people think about yours?

Part of living an extraordinary life means to value self and to take time for the "little things" that make up the big things. Too many are dying of breast cancer, prostate cancer, and complications from diabetes, and other diseases prevalent in certain communities. You cannot be *the gift* if you are not here to live it! Of course, it's easier said than done, but for you there is always help!

Affirmation:
Thank You, God, for filling my spirit, mind, soul, and body with what is suitable to Your taste. Less of me, and more of Thee!

#7 Put God First!

Thank God for your loved ones and for all the good things in your life. When you need something, ask Him. He will always protect, support, and love you. Remember to pray every day, and thank God everyday for YOU!

Psalm 78:35 says, *"And they remembered that God was their rock, and the high God their redeemer."*

In the "Footnotes" of <u>The New Open Bible, Study Edition, (p.755)</u> it is explained,

"To be Holy means to be set apart. God is set apart from the power, practice, and presence of sin, as set apart to absolute rightness and goodness."

My prayer—
Lord, I love You. Thank You for eternal blessings, the ability to think in my right mind, and for another day to serve You. Peace be still. Thank You! In the name of Christ Jesus, Amen.

What do you think?

Taking action is your choice. So, consider specific ways and areas in which you are willing to take action and demonstrate your brilliance. Remember, your divine purpose is extraordinary, and daily you have an opportunity to shine. You are *really* good at something. Find it. Share it. You are needed by people and by God…for the work, for…

the mission of absolute good.

Psalm 27:1 says, *"The Lord is my light and my salvation; whom shall I fear? The Lord is the strength of my life: of whom shall I be afraid?"*

I don't know about you, but I've been "pretty chicken" in my life. Yet showing brilliance is demonstrative. Imagine if we each demonstrate "brightly" each time God calls upon us to service. The concept is extraordinary! Yet, He says it's possible. *Are you listening?*

∞

...*He's calling you to your Extraordinary.*
Remember this passage from #1 Love ...

"Also I heard the voice of the Lord, saying, Whom shall I send,
and who will go for us? Then said I, Here am I; send me."
Isaiah 6:8

Are you willing to answer the call?

Chapter 7

Demonstrating Brilliance in Daily Living
Jo Lena Johnson and Wise Friends

*"A person with a clear purpose will make progress on
even the roughest road. A person with no purpose will
make no progress on even the smoothest road."*
Thomas Carlyle

In each of the interviews I conducted for the *"If You Really Want
to…"* series, as well as this book in particular, I noticed a common
theme almost immediately: every person, not only acknowledged
and embraced a personal spiritual foundation, but also identified it
as a priority in their daily living, the cultivation of a relationship with
God. It also became challenging to separate the *"Seven Ways to Show
Your Brilliance"* into individual numbers because each of these individuals "shine brightly," in several areas and in many of the practices
and principles illustrated throughout the interviews. What a treat for
us! And, what an opportunity to ask yourself what actions you can
take to model behaviors; and what things you can stop doing, if you
have habits which are not in alignment with what you *really want.*

Let's face it. As Christians, we have problems, ups, downs, and conflicts. We are challenged by the effects of culture and society just like
everyone else. Yet, experiences in the face of these circumstances can
be different, if we learn how to discern and how to practice good.

Extraordinary living is a process—not a destination; that's why the book is called *"If You Really Want to...."* Because, if you just *kind of* want to live, then you'll simply read about somebody else's life here. If you *really* want to live, you will begin to analyze, question, examine, and choose, and continue choosing—it's called LIVING!

I personally believe that each time we pass up the opportunity to understand and relate to successful people, we lose wisdom—something we discover in sharing and something we desperately need. Therefore, hear now from some good people who have a few things they *really want to* share...

#1 Love

Honor and Service ~ A Model for Responsibility—
Wisdom from Chief Sherman George

"Do the best you can—and we'll figure out the rest together!"
Chief Sherman George

Chief Sherman George says that they didn't have much when he was growing up, yet their family had the things that they really needed. Because, as a community, people helped each other out by shopping in neighborhood stores for goods and services, relying on each other to be responsible, and by being willing to work. He learned the value of being on time, and "doing your best" every time. Chief George and three of his eleven siblings served in the United States Army. Eventually, he used his G.I. Bill to complete his Bachelor's Degree while he was a husband, a father, and had 5 jobs to support his family because he wanted to earn a living every day he was available.

Chief George says:

"I believe that the ability for men to support the family spiritually, emotionally, and with loving care are crucial to the health and habits of a firm foundation."

Chief George has been married to his wife, Catherine since August of 1971, years he credits God as the first key for their solid foundation and long lasting marriage. The second key, he says, is "My wife is always right!" While raising three daughters together as parents, they raised their commitment to the marriage and to love. They raised their commitment to create a support system of immediate and extended family, along with good neighbors and friends. He believes these things contributed to their daughters' maturity and solid foundation needed for the future.

At the very mention of "granddaughter," his refined countenance changes to the warm glow of a man who absolutely adores these "present moments" in his accomplished and *extraordinary* life. Being a grandfather is a role that he not only takes seriously, but also adores. With a smile he says, "She loves Paw-Paw—she's always nice, well-mannered, intelligent, and those are the basic things."

His granddaughter is sixteen years old and played tennis in the Ukraine for three months in 2009. After that, she spent a few weeks in St. Louis, before returning home to Florida where she lives with her parents.

Chief George:

"I'm so proud of my daughter and my son-in-law for raising her right." He then sighs, *"There are so many kids with so many issues…I feel so sorry for them because I know they could do better if they had the proper*

support. *They need love, and you can't fool kids with "I love you" when you really don't love them; it shows. There is no doubt about it."*

He continued the train of thought by saying that children need the stability of family, and fathers play a big part in achieving that stability. In order to create a sound family environment and, thus, a sound society, men must be skilled and have the opportunity to have good jobs and careers, which allow them to "take care" financially. For the strength that men are always expected to have in the midst of adversity, men need someone and something to help them do better.

Several things I tell myself when I face challenges:

"I'll work harder!"
"I might not be treated fairly."
"I can't fall on my knees and forget about it!"
"I Advocate the 3P's of Success—
Preparation, Persistence, Patience."
—Chief George

In 1847, The City of St. Louis Fire Department was founded, but it was not until 1999 that the Department appointed Chief Sherman George. He worked hard. He had proven himself as skilled, competent, and ready for the responsibility. Of course, he was probably ready sooner than the end of thirty-two years. That was the number of years the Chief had served when he became the first African American Fire Chief in the Department's history. As in his service to the community as one of many firemen, service as "Chief" highlighted his dedication in teaching hundreds of new recruits and seasoned veterans the *3P's of Success* that had always worked for him— Preparation, Persistence and Patience. During forty years of service, those who worked with him as colleague or under his command were equipped to handle extraordinary feats because of his attitude and character. What had brought him to this point was more than plain hard work, expert skills, and persistence. Where these ended, principles of patience, pride in the job, service to others, and faith in God always filled the gaps.

He says:

"I think people should do right based on their belief in God and serving others. Others include your family, church, and community; and serving requires your sacrifice in order to do so. As a public servant for 40 years, it wasn't for them to serve me; it was for me to serve them. I believe I achieved success because I served people."

Extraordinary Results Come from Being Extraordinarily Responsible:

- *Be willing to say, "I messed up;"*

- *Admit mistakes;*

- *Be willing to learn from the past and in making new choices in the future;*

- *Don't make excuses—say, "Hey, let's just straighten it out!"*

- *Some people want to overlook responsibility—don't be one of them;*

- *People want to act like they "don't know" just to stay "hands off"—don't fall into that pattern;*

- *Believe in your purpose and higher calling of service. If you don't yet know what it is, keep learning. Discover it;*

- *Give people the best of who you are in helping them show the best they can be.*

#2 Be Patient and Kind

Mastery and Humility ~ A Jazzy Legacy—
Wisdom from Dwayne D. Bosman

"Learn to be patient; have endurance; keep a 'never give up attitude;' and be able to deal with rejection. If you can do these things, you will be successful in life."
Dwayne Bosman

Dwayne Bosman is a product of good home training. Coming from a strong family foundation, he is grateful for the pride, life lessons, and love that he and his siblings received while growing up. He is the eldest brother of Cheryl D.S. Walker and his twin brother, Dwight, whom he affectionately calls "Little Twin," because he was born 10 minutes later.

Soul-stirring and exhilarating touch the surface of the experience one has when witnessing the performance of these Ambassadors of Music. Known from hometown St. Louis to London and beyond, the Bosman Twins are classically trained musicians, music teachers, and Emmy Award winning Jazz greats.

Dwayne plays eight Woodwind Instruments and credits his parents with providing not only the talent, but also the love, discipline, and grounding to become extraordinary in their craft—and in the opportunity to reach people around the world through their music.

Dwayne Bosman Shares:

"My dad, Lloyd Smith, taught my brother and me to play when we were 10 years old. I started on flute and Dwight started on Clarinet. My dad was from the "Big Band Era" and played with Count Basie, Duke Ellington, Lionel Hampton, Eddie Randle and the Blue Devils, and George Hudson."

"My father invested his time and talent in us, teaching us to love and respect the art and craft of music and that the show must go on at all times. I thank God that he was willing to do that."

Questions Asked of Dwayne Bosman:
How do you feel about music?

"I love it. You have to love it in order to play—as a musician, if you don't; you are wasting your time because it takes dedication. There are musicians who don't love what they do, and it shows. And, in order to make jazz a career, one must really have a passion for it because the financial/monetary reward is not necessarily as great as it is in other music genres."

"I also find great joy in teaching private music lessons. I'm grateful for the investment our parents made in us and to be able to help young people learn how to become skilled musicians. It's an honor to do this. To help the younger generation develop mastery in music is to help prepare them for living and being extraordinary."

Five Things <u>Learning</u> Music Taught Me:

1. Discipline

2. Preparation

3. Individual work study

4. Group work study

5. How to listen—in order to get or learn anything, you must first listen—so developing listening skills.

"Our mother, Paula Smith, was a very accomplished woman as well. She earned degrees from Washington University and also from St. Louis University; she did graduate work at Harvard. She was really passionate about philanthropy and social justice."

"She also instilled in us the importance of civic service, and encouraged our participation in the community and on boards as well."

"I love her, and I appreciate the things she taught and showed us. When we were young, she made sure that she went to church and we went too. She prayed a lot; and she was a humble person herself—which was tough because we were learning to be aggressive and assertive, to be qualified in life and as musicians; yet, she wanted us to remain humble."

My Mother Stressed these Things to Us:

1. To be humble

2. To keep God in our lives

3. To help others

4. To be more about business

How does one deal with rejection?

"You must have faith in God and confidence in yourself."

"Take it with a grain of salt. Naturally, it hurts, but dust yourself off and keep going. It could be about auditioning for a performance or interviewing for a job. It's not always about if you are the best, it may be that someone has an internal relationship with someone, political or whatever. Keep trying because you may be rejected many times before you are recognized. It's part of the process of living. In order to do that, you must have stamina, confidence, and endurance to weather the storm."

"In the meanwhile, you must continue to better yourself because sometimes you may *not* be qualified; so you must keep working until you are."

"The Lord helps those who help themselves and, through God, we can do anything—and we must ask him."

Five Habits that have helped me to be Successful

1. Dependability

2. Professionalism

3. Consistency

4. Being my best

5. Being courteous and humble—never getting to the point that we feel too important. For example, I know that people don't have to come and listen to our concerts or purchase our music.

"Traveling around the world to share my passion for music and for people is not something I take lightly. To have shared the stage with artists like Fontella Bass is an honor. I respect her tremendously. She's "the musician's musician." She's well versed in Gospel and secular music, and my brother and I learned a lot about Gospel music from her—as well as the respect and friendship we shared. Lester Bowie, was a trumpet player and he had several groups. I had a lot of admiration and respect for him because he traveled the world and did what he wanted to do. He placed no limitation on his musical abilities, or his abilities period."

"My siblings and I are creative and hardworking—and we learned this through experience. The dedication and commitment our parents made in teaching us how to learn, how to serve, and how to become skilled is their legacy. It's my goal to continue to share that with people through my actions and our music."

Five Things Teaching Music Taught Me:

1. Patience

2. Endurance

3. To listen to the students carefully—because we can learn from each other.

4. To be better prepared

5. To be more business savvy—in making appointments, scheduling; demonstrating dependability, accountability. And to make clients and audiences feel that it's worth it. All this means "being qualified" as world class.

"I really enjoy teaching music because I know the importance of giving children focus, discipline, and investing in their interests and talent to bring out the best of who they are and can be. I am grateful to God for His many blessings."

See the Bosman Twins perform on YouTube, to learn more, or to study with Mr. Bosman, go to www.bosmantwins.com.

#3 Respect Yourself and Others

Leadership & Responsibility - Smiling Works—
Wisdom from Christopher Cannon

"I make sure that I acknowledge people especially
when I'm at work—I try to speak to everyone
I see…keeping a smile on my face."
Christopher Cannon, Father and Eighth Grade Teacher

Christopher Cannon is a good friend, brother, son, teacher and motivator. He's been that way since attending high school with me at Riverview Gardens High School in St. Louis, where he was actively involved in sports activities of all kinds and received a Scholarship to Northeast Missouri State University, (now Truman State University) in Kirksville, MO. He obtained a Bachelor of Science Degree in Industrial Management. In addition to becoming a Certified Teacher through the State University of West Georgia, he's completing his Master's Degree at Ashford University.

The thoughtful and loving father of 6th grader Aaron Cannon, Christopher is a middle school teacher in Atlanta, Georgia—the same school that Aaron currently attends. He relishes his active role in Aaron's life including their "normal routine" of weekly scheduled outings, Boy Scout meetings, and getting updates from Aaron about which book he's currently reading. By the way, Aaron was recognized as having read the most books (75) in the first five months of this academic year—whereas most students averaged 5 to 10. They enjoy their daily rides to and from school, and take the time to chat about what things have happened during the day.

As the father of a young son, Christopher Cannon says that if he could, he would "emblazon" three messages to each young man, messages that they would never forget…

1. To instill non-violence—the best way to deal with life is to use intelligence. Become smart enough to come up with a different solution.

2. Be the best man you can be—grounded. Always carry yourself in a positive light so that people will see you and say, "Yes, he carries himself with respect and as a gentleman."

3. Always put God first.

According to Mr. Canon as an educator, Three Things that society could do better to support today's young people:

Promote…

1. Education. Education. Education. I can't say it enough. Even though we are an advanced technological society, we are so behind on all fronts. The kids are not being educated.

They are too much into "quick" and are lacking content, like music—lots of words, nice beats, but no content. They don't understand what's being said to them and how it is affecting their lives;

2. Classroom training for parents. Kids come in and are disrespectful to teachers and fellow students. It is being allowed at home, and they are bringing it into the schools;

3. More emphasis on Family Values. Right now there are many broken families. In my lifetime, I've been fortunate to meet people from different cultures, and I realized that they have bonds and support. However, it's missing for us, and we need to get back to emphasizing family:

    a. Sitting down and having traditions, such as set meal times no matter what. There family members get a chance to enjoy each other, talk with parents or siblings…find out what is happening in their lives daily;

    b. Improvement of social skills; practicing the courtesy to allow each other to talk and the tolerance to allow each other to be;

    c. Teaching independence through responsibility and chores—old fashion chores that bring discipline and order to one's life forever, such as doing dishes, cleaning the room, telephone curfews, and limits on TV (and now, video games and the internet).

Mr. Cannon says, "We don't have a sense of family with everyone gathering at home." He believes that too many kids are raising themselves today, considering the high divorce rates, parents' lack of focus on kids' well-being, and lack of structure in the home. He continues, "They don't have people to talk to, such as grandparents or older adults who would pull them aside and who would give guidance. They don't know because everyone is working, or just otherwise occupied. Meanwhile, children are locked into TV and texting, lacking the social skills to really express themselves and communicate." He adds, "At the middle school level, we have to teach them how to express themselves, problem solve, and to understand why things are and have to be a certain way, or can't be a certain way because they are not learning it at home."

He continues:

"Many teachers are faced with "red tape," in that sometimes students need to be parented—with rules, values, and expectations for success, along with accomplishments. When parents don't take time to love, guide, and provide home training, it cheats children and their peers, as well as makes it difficult for schools to educate children. More and more, committed educators are finding it challenging when parents don't recognize opportunities of growth for their kids and for themselves as parents. Now, when parents are having trouble disciplining their children and the children can call and report abuse, a certain amount of power is being taken away from adults to correct destructive behavior."

Mr. Cannon thinks we must concentrate on encouraging youth to get involved in activities, such as scouting. "The Boy/Girl Scouts are great opportunities for growth. These experiences can be further enhanced if parents also get involved. Adults, and especially parents, can be examples in helping them learn to be respectful and responsible people. Children learn real world experiences. They can learn in talking about God and Country, respect, government, ideals, freedoms, and in the unparalleled freedoms and rights we have in the United States. Allow the opportunities; find a way to draw them in. We have freedom of speech, and the opportunity to work and earn a good living, guide our youth in not throwing it away."

According to Mr. Canon, "As long as the individual has will and perseverance, we can get up and make it happen. Youth organizations teach children leadership skills, how to push through challenges, and to 'finish what you start.' In that setting of working with other people—along with a good mix of friends, interests, focus, and the ability to communicate—children are introduced to great practices in achieving *extraordinary* living."

#4 Good Character

"Be Winners, Not Quitters"
A Teacher's Note to Parents
Ni-Rita Baker-Bradford, Veteran Educator

"Be tenacious, strong willed, positive minded, and
spiritual—and you can, and will, make it."
Ni-Rita Baker-Bradford

Mrs. Baker-Bradford says:

"I became an educator fresh out of college in December of 1976; I was the first African-American teacher to integrate the St. Louis' Riverview Gardens School District in January 1977. For 29 years,

I worked with students in 7th-12th grades, teaching a class simply called "English." I was engaged in the teaching and learning process, working directly with students. I taught writing, literature, speaking, and critical thinking skills. In 2006, in another area district, I became an Instructional Coach and Curriculum Specialist for Pre-Kindergarten through 12th grade, which means that I now work with teachers to improve the quality of instruction. The purpose is to raise the engagement level of students, to work with lesson plan designing, and to model activities and assessments.

Presently, I am ready to get back into the classroom and teach again. I like the structure of a school setting because students are there most of the day. I need to be where I can help shape their minds so that they can be productive citizens—after all, they spend 12 years there to learn how to survive. The home environment can create a barrier when they don't come from a stable or loving environment. That's why it's important for teachers to wear many hats. As teacher, you might have to be aunt, uncle, or friend because the kids need it."

Questions Asked of Mrs. Baker-Bradford:
What are some things that people Really need to know about many 21st Century students/youth?

1. They are technologically savvy—they know technology like experts.

2. They are more "street smart," they want to do things pertaining to street life, things that are social. They are bombarded with a sense of violence and strong cultural influences, and education is not a priority for many youth. It has become secondary.

3. Youth have no fear of authority because they compete with authority. They have the attitude that they are just as grown as the person in the position of authority.

4. Many have little self-respect and little respect for others.

5. Many are not goal setters at all—they like to be entertained more than anything. For them, it looks like fun; it's life right now: It's like, "Whatever I do, I do it for now."

"To reach them, you have to be witty, charming, flexible, and creative in your parenting, teaching, and leadership style. You must be youth-centered and less teacher-centered. The teacher is a facilitator—you get them started at the beginning of class, model the skill, and let them do it and then, it has to be at their own pace. If you don't, they easily get frustrated and quit."

What are three things you Really want parents to know?

1. Become more actively involved in your children's interests and their decision making process.

2. Display love daily.

3. Be their first teachers for EVERYTHING. Don't let "the streets" teach them. Don't let the television or the media teach them. Don't let their peers teach them. Become parents as their "first teachers" all over again. You teach them. That is the role a parent should have in a child's life. Act it out!

If parents ignore what you've said, what is likely to happen?

"Children who are mildly misbehaving will become incorrigible and perhaps even criminal-minded for lack of discipline from the home."

Many parents complain about their kids, and many don't play active roles in their lives—and can justify their reasons. What do you say to that?

"It's unavoidably a sacrifice to be a real parent. You sacrifice everything for your child. Your child must come first; your wants and desires should be secondary. You have to be a nurturer as a parent. You, too, must wear many hats to meet every need and every demand of the child. And above all, you must be a role model. You are whom they see."

"Children will mimic, do what you do. Most likely, if they see you smoke (legal or illegal substances), they will too. If they see you dating many partners (overnight, at your home or away from your home), they will too. If they see you 'cussin' and 'fussin' (in the house or in the car), they will do it too. Face it; we have all witnessed or know of such scenes. Make sure you are guiding them by example. In other words, Parents, you need to be the role model, the *extraordinary* example for your children. Don't leave it to the outsiders—entertainers, athletes, and rappers. Those outside the home and community are sadly the usual choices."

What are the top four things people in the Church Community could do to Support Families with Children?

1. Provide role models through sponsored activities.

2. Provide outside resources.

3. Sponsor or offer counseling.

4. Mentor youth and young adults.

"Sometimes parents don't understand, or are not equipped to deal with some of the challenges their children face. If a child is deemed learning deficient, bi-polar, or faces other problems, the child and family need help to manage and overcome. If the community and/or the church provide practical solutions to the family as appropriate, it could be strong support during the recovery period."

What do you say to church leaders of today?

Society and the church must become a support mechanism to families. You must be resourceful. You must interactively provide guidance and leadership in practical ways. You must provide access to Spirituality. You must be a strong force in the community, and you must become a safe-haven for problematic people. Instead of turning people away, people should be able to come to you and find the help they need.

Words of Encouragement to Parents:

"Be tenacious, strong willed, positive minded, and spiritual—and you can, and will make it." You will have challenges. Let the challenges be the opportunities to do something greater, rather than giving up and throwing in the towel. If you put the four things together (see above), it will give you the added resources needed to deal with your children."

"Don't be a quitter—be a winner!"

#5 Be a Willing Student

From Magna Cum Laude to Corporate Leadership
Wisdom from Cecil W. Johnson, III

*"Leadership is courage to confront yourself and others,
and to make adjustments that benefit both."*
Cecil W. Johnson, III

Cecil W. Johnson, III was born in the summer of 1967. He and his younger brother, Kevin were raised by their parents, Cecil, Jr. and Irene (who recently celebrated their 50th wedding anniversary). He graduated from Central High School in Philadelphia, and then attended college at Hampton University where he majored in Business Management. Cecil met his wife Shawna at church, and they are parents to seven-year-old Cecily and four-year-old Ellis.

Questions Asked of Cecil Johnson:
What did it take from you to graduate Magna Cum Laude from Hampton University?

1. Focus

2. Discipline

3. Self-awareness

What is your current title?

"Director, Learning Strategy and Leadership Development for Centocor, Ortho Biotech, Inc., A division of Johnson & Johnson."

That's a pretty big title, what do you actually do?

"I take care of

1. Growing the leaders (competencies) at all levels in the sales and marketing organization;

2. Developing the organizational strategic plan for organizational learning;

3. Measuring the impact on the human capital and business results."

What's your definition of leadership?

"Leadership is courage to confront yourself and others, and to make adjustments that benefit both."

How did you come to that?

"I began with myself. One of the biggest challenges in leadership is self-awareness, and you have to have the courage to take a look at yourself and your flaws."

Why?

"Because it's easier to look outside for the reasons why things aren't going well, as opposed to looking at ourselves…also it is about looking at yourself and understanding your strengths, too. Many times people aren't self-aware enough to know how to flourish."

Many bright, fairly young people in corporate positions have had challenges, when dealing with supervisors and bosses, especially from older generations. What would you say to them?

"Remember that you are there to learn not there to "prove." When we get into a situation and we want only to prove, it may create conflict."

Why is training important?

"It is a venue for learning. If you ask people the question, "Is learning important?" No one would say, "No it's not." However, when you say "training," people may think of either negative experiences or that the training 'is something that the company or someone is making me do;' or the ego says, 'I don't need it.' "

"Yet, the more you learn and apply, the more you are able to differentiate yourself from others and make a larger impact in what you do, and, reach your goals, if you have them."

What are the effects of lack of training in the workforce?

1. Diminishing organizational competencies.

2. Perceptions of lack of commitment to the employee—lower employee engagement.

3. A competitive disadvantage for the individual.

4. Inability to adapt to the changing external environment.

What are your personal habits—things as a youthful executive, husband, and father that you "must do" everyday?

1.   Make my kids lunch.

2.   Express love and compassion to my wife and kids.

3.   Do my work to a high degree.

4.   Focus on the success and development of the people whom I supervise.

5.   Express and give thanks for my God given gifts and life.

I hear your balancing work, home, and family—anything else?

"I stay in touch with my friends regularly. They are important to me because they keep me grounded, humble, and happy; and they keep me focused. Above all, friends keep me serving since having a friend is constantly give and take. There is always some way or some time when I have to be thinking about how I can help them …because that's what they are doing for me."

If you had known something back when you first started your corporate career, what would you have wanted to understand, or do differently?

"My *today* answer is "Lessons…about myself" I would have realized how much power I actually had in being me. I would have focused on and learned more about my strengths and what I bring to the table. I would have realized sooner the positive things people do see in me versus the things people don't see in me."

Why does that matter?

"Because it would have put me more on the offensive early on in life vs. the defensive, since only on the offensive could I truly reach my goals."

As you and I know, we met because you challenged a client to provide more diversity when providing training services. Why did you step up and do that?

"I did so for two reasons:

1. Because I felt that clients and those in our organization deserve to see strong, highly qualified diverse people delivering content that would change their lives;

2. Because I want to give them even more exposure to the world versus the same type of people coming in all the time."

Thank you for that! One last thing… You mentioned your parents celebrated their golden wedding anniversary in the fall of 2009; How was that experience for you?

"My brother and I, and our families arranged their celebration. I was proud, and it made me realize what we should do for older people. It wasn't about giving them money or gifts. Honor is the gift that we really wanted to give them."

#6 Practice Personal Care

Hollywood Music: Creating "The Urban Buzz"
Wisdom from Kevin Fleming

*"Being successful is hard work; it doesn't happen overnight;
it's not popcorn —and there's no such thing as "Reality TV."*
Kevin Fleming

People are often enamored with what they see on the big screens, small screens, and hear on the radio. Media can be a huge launch pad and the worst nightmare. Then, there are the people behind the scenes who make it happen. The people who are the true "reality" behind what we see and hear. Kevin Fleming is one such person.

An entertainment industry veteran, Kevin Fleming is one of the "best guys I know." He knew of his life's passion when he was in high school. It must have been something in that Minneapolis water that directed his friends and him to their destinies. His classmates included Prince and Morris Day, a phenomenal circumstance! Kevin has spent a lifetime not only learning the ropes, but also teaching others how to *not just survive, but also thrive.* He's held some prestigious positions and seen many people rise and fall as a result of changes, challenges, and pure diligence.

Kevin has worked with some of the best in the business. As Vice President/General Manager at Perspective Records, owned by Jimmy Jam and Terry Lewis, he managed artists, recording projects, developed national tours, and acted as the executive producer of music videos. Kevin has also served as Program Director for several of Los Angeles "hottest" radio stations.

Knowledgeable, resourceful, and a dedicated family man, I *really* respect and admire Kevin because he's a leader who *really* cares. It is through his investment in my development that I experienced my first "director level" position—not to mention the "reclamation" of my job, of which you'll learn more about later in the book. —Jo Lena Johnson

Kevin Fleming Shares:

The music business and especially radio has changed so much in the past decade or so, just like many industries around the world. What "survival tips" do you recommend, which might support people in transitioning from what was, to what could be?

"While you are in it, you have to keep your head up and your eyes open. You have to be aware of the business and where it is going. Being able to see and forecast changes before they came were helpful in my being prepared for the next opportunity or the next challenge. These are some other things you have to do specifically in this business, such as…

- Keep an eye on emerging and developing businesses and opportunities. Always be ready to take the skills that you have and be able to transfer them into greater growth areas.

- Communicate and network with friends and colleagues during the time that you have a job and are doing well. This creates an opportunity for advancement and placement when you don't as long as there are people doing the same thing."

"My experiences in radio led me to look at it from the other side of the desk, and it spurred an interest to look at the record side. I was able to experience the recording process, marketing, sales, and artist development, and those things were made available. Promotions led me to do A&R, although it wasn't really my interest."

"Then, I went to General Management, where dealing with a few companies growing, developing my skill set, took me to the VP Level. I made records and traveled around the world before getting back into radio. When the business really started changing, companies were selling off properties (radio stations). Our station was also sold so I was looking for another opportunity. So, I went into the magazine business. I was able to take my communication skills from the record and radio side and use all the skills I had developed to do so successfully."

"Transitions happen all the time. My publication started as a weekly fax communiqué between radio and the urban music community, as a snapshot of what's going on in the business. It turned into a PDF delivered newsletter and website; and now it's a weekly eblast."

"People are on the go, and they want a fast "headline news" type of thing. We try to give a quick snapshot—information that is a consolidated quick read. In this business, information is essential if you are an executive on the radio side, record side, or even if you are coming up in the business and you want to be "in the know," it's a must have."

What are some "Survival Tips" for this changing Career Climate?

"Well, not everybody is able, or willing, to jump in at the deep end of the pool, so sometimes the best way to swim is to wade into the water. Look at your current situation and environment; and look at where you are and what you can do to improve your situation right where you are. If you find yourself "out," think about what you know and whom you know. Then, transition to where you want to be. Think: Where can you get help with where you want to go? Remember...

1. Being prepared is the most important thing, which includes
   - Tightening relationships;
   - Organizing your thoughts; and
   - Keeping your resume current.

You never know when you'll need to make a change or call on someone. And, if you're not changing, you are being left behind."

The "Top of the Charts" List from Kevin Fleming on Wisdom:

1. People need to find their passion. I was able to go into a field I was extremely passionate about, made the decision, and took the steps, back in high school. I have also been able to help people discover and grow into good employees and good people.

2. You must like what you do. It's hard to be successful if you don't like it. Putting in energy is one of the best and worst things if you work for yourself. You may not know about quitting time, but know how to ration playtime. Still, stay focused.

3. Be diligent and have "thick skin." Producing good work is a process of repetition. You must keep asking. You never know when someone will say "yes."

4. Relax and recharge. You must stay humble. For example, my newsletter doesn't have my name in it. I didn't want it to be about me. When you try to be the news and be bigger than the news, you have problems.

5. Your word must mean something. Integrity is important, and there's a great value in helping people. I try to work on karma. Sometimes I do things for people, and I don't tell them that I will do it. I don't expect them to do something back. I get it back in what I do one way or another, and I think the universe will take care of me.

6. Cherish your children. My son is special to me, and it is a challenge, since he looks to me as a role model. Children do what you do, not what you say. Your actions will be emulated by them. It's very important to understand and keep that in mind when you have them in your presence… in your life, near or far.

7. Drugs and alcohol are easy. There are people who want what they want, but understand that you can't be wide-eyed and open to anything. There are people who will take advantage. That's something you have to learn through experience; it's not really something that people can teach you.

8. Marriage can work in Hollywood! I've been married 25 years, and I have a very supportive spouse who, not only understands the challenges I face but tries to help me overcome them. You really need someone who is in your corner, who can see things with a different view, with a different eye; who can check you into reality. That's one of the great things about being married and having a spouse who is not directly involved in the business.

"Being successful is hard work; it doesn't happen overnight; it's not popcorn and there's no such thing as "Reality TV"—that's a TV show. Success is what happens when you are by yourself and you look in the mirror and say, 'I'm being true to myself.' "

"Your time will definitely come, if you can say, "I am being a good person." Trying to be positive and doing right by your friends and family—that does make you proud of you. If you can say, 'Yes, I'm doing that,' then you are doing all right."

To learn more about Urban Radio or to receive Consultation about successfully navigating through the Music Industry, Reach Kevin Fleming at editor@theurbanbuzz.com.

#7 Put God First

A Collegiate Journey to the NFL
Wisdom from Daryl E. Whittington

"Don't ever let a man tell you what you cannot do—even if I tell you."
Daryl Whittington

One day last fall, in preparation for a youth project, former NFL Player and University of Missouri-Columbia Graduate, Daryl Whittington, agreed to meet and speak with Jonathon Terry—a young man who grew up in my neighborhood. Daryl has shown extraordinary focus:

Daryl received a full athletic scholarship to the MU and graduated with a Bachelor of Science Degree in Environmental Design and a Master of Science Degree in Architectural Studies. Furthermore, he is a recipient of the Don Faurot "Most Inspiring Player Award" for Leadership, and he has played for National Football League's Philadelphia Eagles, the NFL Europe's Frankfurt Galaxy 2003 World Bowl Champions, and for the Canadian Football League's Toronto Argonauts.

Daryl is committed to preparing today's youth through communicating with them directly, as was the case with Jonathan, and also through hosting his radio program on a local St. Louis radio affiliate.

A question asked in the interview was, "what he'd like to share" with a young man interested in attending his Alma Mater (MIZZOU). There Daryl had excelled academically by being the first "athletic student" to graduate with a degree in Architecture, while also participating in MU's football program.

He had plenty to share with Jonathon, and I'm grateful to have been there to capture the interview so that we can all benefit.

Daryl Whittington Shares:

Preparing Young Men for Success

- "You must be "coachable." It's hard to be a good leader, if you don't learn how to accept direction from those in authority and respect people, like your coach. It's not what you say; it's what you do that gets people's attention."

- "'I know it all' is the WRONG Attitude to have!"

"The most important "Three Books" to help you be a successful athlete are:

1.   The Good Book (Daily study of the Bible)

2.   The Academic Book(s). (Disciplined commitment to master school work)

3.   The Play Book (Taking care of assigned duties and following instruction in order to do your job as a member of the team)."

"You must cultivate yourself as a person. If you bring the discipline, knowledge, and growth from study and application of the 'Books' above, you will place proper priority on other aspects of your life. While I am a proud member of Kappa Alpha Psi, Fraternity, Incorporated, and was a member of several other organizations, I was able to enjoy and have fun because I knew my commitment to God came first."

"Hard work, dedication, and commitment, along with altruism, are the core essentials of being successful on and off the playing field.

• Altruism—is the unselfish concern for the welfare of another. You have to realize that in life there is something greater than you are. Playing sports gives you an opportunity to be a part of something much greater than yourself, and it gives you an opportunity to become great at what you do.

• It's not good enough to hit the homerun in the game and then ignore what's happening in real life. Making winning plays should happen in business, in the home, and in the church."

"You have to pass the 3:00 am test—short, simple, and precise.

If you want to be great, it's the small details that separate the good from the great. By achieving your objectives, you will excel on the field and in the game of life."

"And, Remember: Don't put all of your eggs in one basket—have a backup plan for sports and in life.

Work ethic (discipline) sets most people apart. It is the foundation for *extraordinary* living. Most top athletes became 'top' because of their work ethic—not simply because they were 'born with talent.' I believe that most Hall of Famers would have been extraordinary in other disciplines, even if sports were not at play…"

Daryl continues:

"Yet, being involved, prepared, guided, and willing provides the fertile ground for extraordinary living. If you choose sports, be clear on your priorities and get your degree. It's a mindset of finishing what you have started, and it's a known fact that NFL Players with college degrees have 50% longer football careers and make more money, on average, than those who didn't graduate."

"But, seek first the Kingdom and all His righteousness."
Matthew 6:33

SECTION FOUR: CHURCH LIFE—THE GOOD, THE UNSIGHTLY, AND THE TRUTH

Chapter 8

Behaving as a Minister—About Your Words and Actions
Dr. Lee Roy Jefferson

"If you give these instructions to the believers, you will be a good servant of Christ Jesus, as you feed yourself spiritually on the words of faith and of the true teaching, which you have followed."
1 Timothy 4:6 (Good News Translation)

They Call Me Dr. Jefferson...

Many times they call people "reverend" however, people call me Dr. Jefferson. The distinction, "Reverend" is a position of respect in the ministry, and "Dr." is a position of respect and honor in terms of achievement.

The way I carry myself versus the way some ministers carry themselves...sometimes you don't know if they are serious or not serious, it is engrained in me. I took my vows, in terms of being a

Minister of Jesus, seriously, which means I don't act foolishly and carry on foolishly like many other ministers.

Instead of saying things directly, they may be indirect and try to create humor; appealing to the people's sense of humor (for the human selves). There are some who want the congregation to see them as human, not as a person who is deeply sacred and religious. What I seek to do is *to balance*: I'm relatable to people, and, at the same time, I distance myself from some things so that I won't be mischaracterized or not taken seriously.

I Graduated from Hungerford High School 1964 near Wharton, Texas (about 60 miles south of Houston). Out of high school, I went to Wharton County Junior College with a concentration of industrial arts (building furniture, using wood)…I thought one day I would have a garage and build big stuff; it hasn't happened yet, though I have made a lot of jewelry boxes and birdhouses!

I then received a full scholarship to East Texas Baptist College in Marshall, Texas, where I planned to pursue a degree in history (I sometimes wish I had stayed in history). During that summer at Wharton County Junior College, I was a missionary scholarship student (thanks to Texas Baptist Student Union) at Mount Zion Baptist Church in Los Angeles, California. My mentor there was Dr. Hill, who advised me NOT to go to East Baptist, which was just opening to black students. He suggested that I to go to Bishop College.…I had never heard of it, that predominately-black college.

Dr. Hill felt my ministry would be predominately to black families; and, even though I would work and have relationships with those who were not black, it would assist me to have the *foundation* of Bishop College for my future. While I respected his opinion, a scholarship awaited me and, at the scheduled time, I went to East Texas in Marshall and arrived to campus by bus.

I was on campus for eight hours, and, for some reason, I did not like campus or the environment. So I went to the Dean's office and informed him that I would be leaving the school. I thanked him for the opportunity and for the scholarship, he was spellbound about my leaving; yet, he reluctantly accepted, my words and a said, "I wish God's blessings on whatever you do."

I left the office, without mentioning my destination, got my things, and made my way back to the bus station in Marshall. That night around midnight, I took a bus and arrived in Dallas about 6:00 am the next morning. I had no appointment, no meeting, and I had no discussion with anyone about attending Bishop College. I asked around and found that there was a local bus that would take me to the college. I went to the administrative building on campus, and, as I was entering, a man walked out of the building named Mr. Hogan. I didn't know him, and he didn't know me. Mr. Hogan said, "Young man, are you willing to work while you go to school?" and I said, "Yes!" He invited me to his office, he was Director of Placement at Bishop College!

Without delay, he signed me up to work at the United States Post Office. Incidentally, this is the same post office located directly across the street from where Oswald shot President Kennedy, I was working the night it happened. I remember when the word came that he had been shot, and they had rushed him to the hospital. He was in grave condition and everyone was saddened. We said a word of prayer for him. Later that night, we heard that he had died.

…I graduated from Bishop College in Dallas, Texas.

I Say, Young Ministers, That...

The priority is education and training—to build Christian Education; and then it's the Christian Education that builds the church. The priority will be to evangelize (the process of bringing people into the church), to train, and equip, growing people up in the Word and teaching the Word of God and repeating that process over and over again. That was the formula in primarily white churches in the past. They wouldn't get out and build a big building; they would build Christian Education. As people would join the church, they were winning souls and equipping them through Sunday School, and Bible Study. They had training of members and leaders, classes for leaders and for members.

The same concept was applied in my community with farmers when I was growing up in Texas. The farmer would go out and build a large barn with all the equipment needed to build the barn. Once he had the building to operate the farm, then he concentrated on all the equipment that would help him to build the house or the *dream* house for the family. But, until that time, the farmers and their families lived in moderation...

> *"Christian Education in Ministry includes*
> *Personal Development, Church Direction,*
> *and Addressing Human-Felt Needs."*
> Dr. Lee Roy Jefferson

Speak to inform or educate the present generation about how you've been lead and blessed and how, if they allow God to lead and guide their lives, they can have a similarly rewarding experience.

"Love the LORD Your God...
These are the commands, decrees, and laws the LORD
your God directed me to teach you to observe in the
land that you are crossing the Jordan to posess."
Deuteronomy 6:1 (NIV)

Consider your Actions

1. **Commit your life to reading the word of God daily.** Do you know when it's time for a minister to retire? When he reaches a point where he does not want to do any reading; then it's time. The heart of ministry is just reading. There are too many ministers who don't read.

2. **Walk and live in a respectable manner.** Live in a manner that honors God, you and others. Don't come down to meet others in terms of behavior; reach out and lift them up.

3. **Give thought to the other side.** You cannot lead people when you socialize with them in an inappropriate way outside of the church. Because the truth is, only the people who *really* know you can hurt you.

4. **Love the people.** You need to do this as a leader, as a minister. You must have a heart, have a mind, and have sensitivity for the people's lives and their situation. Some ministers don't see people, except on Sunday. Maslow's "Hierarchy of Needs" says that love is a strong thing. If you are called to a people, assigned to a people, you must have the love, passion, and heart for it. And, if you don't, I don't think you need to do it. You are assigned, called to do it. It is a service, and your *joy* is in doing the work.

*"May the favor of the Lord our God rest upon us; establish the
work of our hands for us—yes, establish the work of our hands."*
Psalm 90:17 (NIV)

Most organizations employ the principles of accountability, roles, job
expectations and all of that…but we often think more of the heart
rather than the head, when it comes to the Black church. I've found
that sometimes ministers don't consider what's *really* important.
Many times the choices that church leaders make are not issues of
money; they are *really* issues of priorities. It's important to be clear—
especially when it comes to providing a foundation for fortifying the
church—the people, practices, and ability to make good decisions
build a foundation for Christian Education.

Chapter 9

Keys to Building a Successful Ministry Include Passionate Service
L. Jefferson and J. Johnson

"Christian Education is Key to Building a Successful Ministry."
Dr. Lee Roy Jefferson

Young Ministers, keep in mind when preparing for the work of Christian Education that:

1. Being loyal to certain people, at the expense of other people, is not a good practice.

2. Uplifting and upgrading the teachers of the church, in terms of treatment and compensation, will insure that you get the most qualified and passionate people to help you grow your ministry.

3. Getting the right people in place is essential for your ministry. A ministry needs people and sound finances.

4. Not every avenue that leads to growth in membership and expanded finances is necessarily a positive impact on sound ministry and Christian Education.

When we make teaching Christian Education priority, you will see a change. An organization that's not training or teaching will not prosper.

Quality, Preparation, and Training

Churches must be centers of Spiritual activity, integrity, and order. To fulfill the call of God and to properly serve His people, it is the Pastor's responsibility to employ people who are not only loyal and committed to serving in the church, but who are also qualified to function in the capacity for which they were hired. Too often, the church is filled with "old friends, loyal buddies," those who would be perfectly comfortable keeping things the way they "have always been." In order to *really* reach the people, you must rise to the times—with the willingness to embrace technology, resources, programs, and qualified people who can help keep the church vibrant, relevant and on point. Too often leaders would rather give the orders rather than "hear from their people" about what they could personally do better. Being a good steward is also about obedience and cooperation.

When you are in search of an assistant or a "Right Hand," it's important to choose someone with certain qualities and strengths. You will have expectations of that person, and they will have expectations of you. Much is required of you, and here is a list that should help you in building your relationship with your own "right hand."

Requests from a "Right Hand" to Pastors

1. **We Need Trust and Honesty**: I need this with anyone with whom I work—and especially you. Please be open in your communication, be clear about what you need, and then trust me to represent you in your absence—it's my pleasure to be your right hand.

2. **Please Plan Ahead and be Forthcoming**: When you give me the information I need, I can do my job in excellence for

example, knowing in advance if time is going to be taken off, knowing about certain meetings, and knowing about scheduling of all kinds. It helps me to be able to make the best arrangements. When I have a feeling for what the meeting is supposed to be about, I can get things arranged.

3. **Please Be on Time**: When you're not on time, it can cause confusion, delay, and it shows others that it's okay for you to be late. It also shows them that they can be late as well. It's not purposeful or a good use of resources.

4. **Let's Handle our Business with Qualified People**: As your "right hand," I also serve to reach across all Ministries to make sure the programs get done in an efficient manner, in excellence. We must be willing to break some of the old traditions of putting people in certain positions because they are willing to volunteer, are agreeable, or have the time. I want to serve in *extraordinary* ways and with training, tools and co-workers who are bright, energetic, and skilled, at whatever age. They are the best choice. Good salaries for good service will be excellent investments in the life and development of our church.

Skill Set Needed For This Type of Work

1. **Must be Confident that God has put you in the place.** The individual will run up against obstacles in the natural and the only place you can really deal with them, is through God.

2. **Must be Able to Project/to Communicate the Pastor's Heart.** The individual must be the kind of person who deals with people in a certain way and then be able to communicate with them in the same way, joyful, glad-hearted, but firm.

3. **Must be able to Deal with Adversity in a Kind Manner.**

4. **Must Have Writing Skills.** The individual must write from the mind and heart to communicate clearly and effectively to the ministries in terms of what they need to do.

5. **Must Be Able to Pull Together Volunteers.** One must find people who are doing things, not for pay, and make sure that the job gets done.

Church Leadership must get past the "Can you give me a deal?" Mentality.

Outside of the daily church workers, there are many things that need to be done in the life and activity of the church. Too many pastors work on a "voluntary mentality," meaning that they don't want to pay people for their time and service. While it is important and honorable for people to give back to their church and community, it's not always feasible to ask congregants to provide services without some form of compensation. Nothing is ever free.

Everyone has issues and things they need to pay for; so, when enrolling people to provide goods, services or to drop off or pick up things, please consider that many people are struggling in their personal lives. If the church can give them a small boost and get a valued and needed service at the same time, the quality improves, and we are practicing and showing people abundance.

Preaching is the spoken Truth of God conveyed through the Minister's Personality.

And when that happens, people are standing around talking and don't rush to go home because there is a longing in the worshippers to deepen the moment through conversation and fellowship...When the people don't receive the heart to heart spoken Truth of God's Word, often they leave church quickly after the benediction.

Passionate Service is Your Momentum.

Passionate Service is the unction where information or communication goes from the speaker to the listener, the sense of feeling, conviction, and anointing. What grows the church is when the speaker or leader shows honesty and integrity in such a way that the listener receives the truth.

Passionate Service affects every aspect of your life when you are Committed to Living *Extraordinarily.*

At home, at work, at the grocery store and in every one of your relationships your attitude and behavior are what grow your possibilities or potentials. When people feel your truth and your heart they are more likely to be inspired, motivated or strengthened. Your attitude and actions lay a foundation for building the trust, cooperation, and the relationship.

In order to service the needs of people, you, the leader of your life, must be disciplined, consistently and daily, in your whole life. This requires investing the time, energy, and effort to achieve beyond ordinary measure.

"Service Skills" and treating/training people "up" to standard is imperative. The actions and attitudes needed to *extraordinarily* serve begin with you, as you create the experience for yourself and you set the tone for those whom you meet.

"When you see errors don't just run with it…
Providing good customer service takes an affinity
for people, good training, and survival skills."
Dawn Conner

Being Passionate About Good
Customer Service
Wisdom from Dawn Conner

Dawn Conner grew up in St. Louis and graduated from Rosati-Kain High School in the Class of 1987. During college, she also participated in the INROADS/St. Louis program. The program helped her, as well as other talented students, learn crucial professional development skills during her internship with the Monsanto Chemical Company. She earned her Bachelor of Science Degree in Marketing at Saint Louis University in 1991.

LaMorris Connor is her husband of 12 years, and they have two sons, David, 8 and Chase, 6. Dawn is a customer service "officiando." She is absolutely passionate about fair treatment, good service, and meeting needs. She has been able to merge her passions, her experience, and her devotion to service into a good, if not particularly straight, career track. Like most families, Dawn's family has had its share of transitions, debt, job losses, and some milestones. She says that she and LaMorris pray together to get through heartache and struggles. Dawn says, "We depend on God. He is our source and strength and hope."

Dawn Conner Shares:

"Years ago, our family moved to Dallas with Occidental Chemical Company in the International Customer Service Area, and I was asked by a former counterpart to consider being manager for the team. I did it for 6 months, and, when they offered me a voluntary separation package, I took it."

"After I left there, I applied for different positions and didn't get any hits. I was very active at my church and was asked if I would come and work with the church doing marketing part time. After a year, I became the Director of Assimilation. Assimilation occurs when a person visits the church, goes through the membership process, and gets plugged into ministry. I held the position for seven years."

"In 2006, we returned to St. Louis when my husband had an opportunity to come back to work with a family business. I started my current position in November 2008, and of course, it's in customer service."

Questions Asked of Dawn Conner:
What did you like about your role as Director of Assimilation?

"Several things come to mind:

1. I liked being behind the scenes and meeting needs, which are very important to the goals of the church.

2. I touched and dealt with so many types of people including staff, church members, outside vendors, deacons, ministry leaders, and different people to get things done related to all aspects of church ministry.

3. I was the one in the middle of the wheel, making things happen.

4.   I enjoyed working full time for God and dealing with Godly things. It was great! I was able to do it, get paid for it, and have benefits.

5.   I also went on two mission trips abroad, one to India and then to Peru. It was ministry, and I didn't have to use vacation time!

6.   When people had surgery, I could go to the hospital and pray with them…in the corporate environment, I am unable to do those things."

Now that you've moved back "home" to St. Louis, what are you up to?

"I do International Customer Service for Canada, Europe, the Middle East and Africa, and back up my counterparts who service the rest of the world. God's clock is a whole lot different from ours. My customers are either distributors or agents. I deal with bookings with steamship lines—most things go by ocean versus air…ingredients for food products and other goods."

"I get to solve problems, and there is no day that is typical. And, now that I'm back in 'international,' and my customers are usually asleep when I'm on my way it's mostly email and a lot of paperwork versus being on the phone."

"In International Customer Service, I have to get materials booked on a vessel. If it's going to China, it takes a month; Europe 10 days; and, when Samoa had an earthquake, I had to make a decision if we were still going to ship."

Dawn continues to share:
"There are Five Traits of Good Customer Service...

1. Follow up;

2. Problem solving;

3. Being detail oriented;

4. Organizing; and

5. Servicing/Tending to people by meeting their needs."

"Major Skills Needed to Be Successful in Customer Service...

- Be flexible.

- You have to like dealing with people because they are going to call (on) you. When listening to someone, you can tell if the person is tired, tired that day, or tired of doing it (giving good customer service).

- Use common sense. When you see errors, as a representative you cannot just run with it, such as things on order in error. It might be worth delaying the order to get clarification on what is happening in the process."

"When I go to work, I'm literally on stage, I'm in a performance from the time I get there until the time I leave. It *really* helps to deal with some of the things that are going on. Still, many companies look at customer service as a meaningless task; however, a lot of companies go under because they have poor customer service."

"In order to be successful, you must like dealing with people. And, if you don't have the mindset, you will not survive. It takes survival skills because you will not learn about customer service in school."

"I don't think there is a customer service degree or customer service training in school, but thank God for my INROADS training. I'm also grateful for having the opportunity to work for a company before beginning my actual corporate career."

"The Four Most Valuable Things I learned as an INROADS Intern...

1. I learned how to interact with people on many levels and in many settings. I had opportunity to work in a company for four summers with "business people" assignments and to interface with executives in meetings and activities.

2. The mock interview training, dress for success, and management styles trainings were invaluable.

3. Making real money taught me what it was like to make a real salary, one that paid for my college education. I realized that I was "well off" for an intern. One of my peers bought a Porsche; however, I used my salary to pay for college.

4. It taught me how to network with people, and while involved there I met people who became life-long friends."

"We spent four summers training and being prepared through the college experience. It all helps when starting in the corporate environment and can help you get through that "corporate" experience—which can be something—and not everyone survives it. I miss church work—and I'm grateful that I still have the ability to *serve* God every day of my life."

Chapter 10

Engaging People: Losing People Is Not Extraordinary!

Really? What about "Church"?
L. Jefferson and J. Johnson

"Why condemn the wrong doers in your sermons...give us solutions!"
Monica Dinwiddie

When interviewing people about their thoughts on "Church," the survey was not the best. People shared their thoughts and feelings about the ceremony of church, their views of church, and also reasons why they choose or don't choose to participate in attending church. While it's easy to justify our own behavior, and super easy to pass judgment on others, here are some things for your consideration.

We did a small, targeted survey of people between the ages of 32 to 47 and asked the question, "Why do you/don't you go to church regularly?" We asked this group because they represent the "bridge" between the elders and the youth coming up. They are today's and tomorrow's leaders. They are big influencers of youth because many of them are parents. What they do and don't do affects us all.

The Recent Survey Shows:
Question #1. If you could say one thing to Today's Ministers, Pastors and/or Church Leaders, What would it be and Why?

Aletia Chandler answers:

"*Only one thing? LOL (Laughing on Line). They (we) don't teach discipleship. We talk a lot about what we have in Christ, but don't teach how to live that out practically. It's one thing to say we have freedom from sin and death and to walk in the spirit, etc., but if I'm bogged down with strongholds, I don't know how to live that out practically and, therefore, I'm not truly reflecting God's glory.*

I'm walking around as if I'm still defeated and my behavior hasn't changed much even though I'm now saved. We tend to focus on getting people in the church and getting saved, and then leave them on their own to figure it out after that. We don't guide one another. I hear people saying amen in church and cheering, but then when they leave, they have no idea how to apply the message. They have a desire to know God intimately and live for His glory, but don't really understand why they have not changed."

La Tia King answers:

"*You should always convey that every house of worship is the house of the Lord—not the house of the founder or the house of the leader. Because I hear a lot of times that the minister is the founder, it disturbs me somewhat. Because as a Christian, "Christ is the founder" of every church. Thinking from that standpoint, it sounds as if you are placing yourself on the same level as Christ. On the other hand, I would like to thank you for being a vessel of inspiration to people—keeping them with hope—I know it's not an easy job to lead. But, when you take that capacity, the ones I know, at least, are truly anointed.*"

Corey Jackson answers:

"Because the church is filled with so much hypocrisy at the hands of those who are delivering the Word, it really does raise a brow of suspicion. I have no desire to come into a church to sit back and listen to someone preach about being so godly, only to find that same person preaching is creeping as soon as the service is over. Clearly, this does not apply to all of you clergy folks, but "guilty by association" is a hard rap to beat.

So with that in mind, I personally find that my prayers, faith in God and when and where I decide to get the Word, seems to fit me just fine. And I would question those who would question me about why and how I stay in touch with God outside of the church as opposed to IN the church. After all, I have found that speaking to those close to me who share the same faith beliefs and can understand my struggles, all while providing me with what I need to hear (encouraging and scolding) does me just fine. So…other than being IN church with others like me and others who would look down on me because of my ways…please tell me what I would get from being in church that I am not getting now?"

Letter Submitted from the Survey…

In response to our survey, we received a passionate letter regarding an individual's opinion of some church leaders and their behavior. In order to be true to the intention of this book, which is to assist each reader in practicing extraordinary Christian Living, we must be willing to include the "harsh realities" of today. To illustrate and to move beyond the worldly standards that have dominated and undermined the Truth of God's Word and His purpose for us as teachers, preachers, parents, and citizens—all must raise our thoughts, feelings, behaviors, expectations, and standards.

Too many people are being lost because they cannot get beyond what they see. If we don't set higher, *extraordinary* standards and exemplify them, we are not being obedient to our claims of being "Christians."

Dear Dr. Jefferson and Ms. Johnson:

What I would say to "some" leaders of the church is, "Thank you, but no thank you!"

I've seen preachers/leaders of the church try to tell a lost soul right from wrong, when they are no better than the so-called sinners. They are hypocrites, liars, cheaters, deceivers, and businessmen/women. These are some of the questions I would ask "some" of our church leaders…

Why is it that you preach to me that the casinos and bars are bad, when I've seen you at both of these places shaking the dice, having a drink and looking all happy and glad?!?! (Hypocrite)

Why do you preach about fornication and adultery, when I've witnessed you having babies with your church members, and outsiders, while the first lady is seated on the first pew at the church as if she is not aware? (Cheater, Deceiver)

You preach about battery and abuse of your spouse, when behind closed doors your wife is every name in the book, and hiding bruises.

Why has church become a business? So you can drive around in your Benz/Cadillacs, and wear those fancy suits and shoes to match?

Why do you lead your followers out the church doors when you need to bring them in for spiritual guidance, prayer, and much, much, more?

C-mon, preacher man, I'm lost. Can you lead me? Maybe you can deceive me, free me, take my money, and cheat me.

To all my church leaders that are doing right by the Lord, thank you; I applaud you. I know now that every preacher walks around without a clue.

I'm 32 years old and live in Kansas City, Missouri.

Signed,
Anonymous

Reasons I don't regularly attend church...

1. *"The explanation for the meaning of life, salvation, etc. in the church seems to have a fairy tale ending. It's like "Santa Claus"... you do good, you get a present (go to heaven). I'm not buying that explanation. I believe that if you think you are going to a better place (heaven), you'll treat where you're at like crap.*

    When you go to school and learn math, you start with Arithmetic, then go to Algebra, and on to Calculus. It seems to me that life and the afterlife would be just as complicated as the progression of math classes, but church seems pretty basic and simple with it. There are some books that I take more comfort in with their explanation. There's a ton of good things that come with church, and it helps many people; but I'm not one of them." T.D.B.

2.   *"I don't consider myself a "Christian" anymore. My relationship with God is so much deeper than a denomination. Where I do get my communal/corporate spiritual nourishment from doesn't meet on a regular basis like a Sunday service." O.M.*

3.   *"I just do not go. There may be a reason that I don't go because I haven't taken the time to find a church, but I just don't go. I want to go, but I don't." D.F.*

4.   *"Pure laziness and I have not found a church that inspired me to continue to go. I will say that I am on the hunt locally and will, hopefully, be filled with the spirit that God has to offer. I grew up going to church 3 times a week up until 8th grade and then once a week through most of high school. I have gone through my adult life off and on, but not consistently. I'll get there. I promise!" S.D.*

5.   *"I don't feel comfortable being in there—it's a show, too much entertainment—they have a script to follow; pretty much the first hour you have singing(with) the praise team and if you are lucky, in the last 45 minutes the Pastor comes out to talk. There is a clear difference based on denominations and most of the African-American churches I've gone to, your whole day is gone, after you've listened to the "choir's preachment" versus hearing the Pastor." C.C.*

6.   *"I think people are still caught up in the fashion shows and miss the whole purpose of being at church. What's most important is cutting to the chase and getting what I can get out of it. I'd like to hear what's being presented—things that are relevant to me, to the world and what's going on outside…today, last week, current activities that happened within the past week." C.R.*

7. *"My attention span is short and I don't like being there all day. I appreciate words sung that are relevant to that day, warming the crowd is okay but, I'm more interested in what the Pastor has to say. It's similar to students wanting shorter class times—present what's important and move on." S.M.*

Reasons I do attend church:

1. *"I know that God is everywhere, I can be in the park and be with God, and attending church is more than a habit for me, I enjoy it. Because I need renewal and when I'm in church—having the other people around me, the worship, seeing the minister, experiencing the music, the choir—we are all in the moment together and it seems more powerful—being there seems to forge a deeper connection—it's better than I get at home alone." — Ms. Daryle Brown*

2. *"I don't believe all of this wonderful creation came from nothing or is out of chaos. I believe that God is a God of order and of love that is so supremely beyond what any of us can know on this side of glory, that our sanctification and purification in this life seem like trouble and turmoil when they are really the greatest gift we can have when we accept them. I believe this God has revealed himself in his Word (The Bible and the personal incarnation of Jesus Christ.) and continues to reveal himself to us through His Holy Spirit (that testifies to Jesus and his Word." —Charles Neville*

Pastor Damon Cannon Shares:
Three Practical Reasons to Attend Church

1.   **Spiritual Empowerment:** Even for persons who are not the most "spiritual," it is still beneficial for them to learn the biblical principles and life applications that help us to cope with everyday life.

2.   **Fellowship:** We can all benefit, to some degree, from being in fellowship with others that may not be a part of our immediate family, maybe just to give some different perspective on things that we may be dealing with. Also, we have an opportunity to positively impact others.

3.   **Code:** We all have to identify with some code of conduct, some kind of value system, and church is a good way of establishing a basis for conduct in our lives and for our families. It gives us some fundamental structure and a venue to practice it, as school did for us as children.

Elder Damon L. Cannon serves as Pastor of Ephesus Missionary Baptist Church and is also Pastor and Founder of New Beginnings Church, both located in St. Louis, Missouri. To learn more about the ministry please visit www.unitedbodyofchristministries.com.

Chapter 11

Serving in the Church:
Formal Work and Loyal Service
L. Jefferson and J. Johnson

"Make a joyful noise to the Lord all the earth! Serve the
Lord with gladness! Come into His presence with singing!"
Psalm 100:1–2 (ESV)

Five Things I Love about My Church
from Arlene Gibbs

1. The Word is revered, and it is spoken and given to us from an anointed pastor.

2. The people of the church are serious in their study and their application of the word. For example, when we are doing things for the community, people get outside of themselves and they work hard in the community because that's what God would have them do, give.

3. The location of the church is in the hub of the community; we are a community church. We are trying to face outward from the four walls of the church into the community.

4. We have a heart for children, young people, and education, as it applies to the young people of the church. The fact that when you walk into the church, you hear children, you hear babies crying and "baby talk" and you know that the church is vibrant based on that!

5. The general fellowship that we have demonstrates this is *my* church family. I look forward to seeing them each week, in ministry and worship. I'm proud of my church family."

Sister Arlene Gibbs, Deaconess, and Executive Director of Programs at Metropolitan Baptist Church in Newark, New Jersey, whose Pastor is the Rev. Dr. David Jefferson, Sr., shared this entry about her experience serving in her church.

Five Church Workers talk About Their Service

#1. "Working for the Lord." I must make sure that I continue to keep a relationship with Christ. I must have time to pray and meditate.

#2. "Part of My Calling." As a deaconess, I am supposed to work within a relationship with church members in a way similar to a situation of family counseling. It is a challenging commitment as I move through counseling, to crisis, to baptisms, and other events, activities, and meetings.

#3. "My Top Concerns Today." For me, it is social issues. For example, everyday people need guidance on where to go to get help. Their lives have broken down, and they need to get back on track—including jobs, housing, getting help with family problems, and even sources for health care. I can pray with them and direct them to resources inside the church, or I can negotiate services for them outside the church. Sustaining community people through issues of unemployment is an example.

#4. "Visiting the Sick." After Sunday services I travel with a group from the church to a particular hospital. We may also stop at homes on the route. Those we visit may require communion or ask for prayer (If it is a busy day, sometimes we don't get home until about 5:00 pm.). The people are really so pleased to be with you. We pray with them and leave our cards as greetings and signs that we were there. It's rewarding, and I really enjoy it.

#5. "A Calling on Your Life to Be a Servant." The calling to be a worker—if that is known between you and God, and He makes it known as a revelation to the pastor, you are then chosen.

Formal Church Work is Essential

It's essential because it provides the vision, structure, and perspective for ministry. The leadership is to minister to the inward needs of the church and its members, as well as to the outward needs of the community at large. While we minister to the hearers/believers inside the church, our Divine Commission as Christians is to the world.

Formal church work is the heart or frame to do the ministry. It's where people are brought together to receive, to know, and to be directed in areas of need. For example, many people experience financial challenges, illness, and displacement due to various disasters, breakups, or job losses. Through individuals making the church aware of the needs, the church can and should respond.

Discipleship is building up individuals through teaching, worship, study, and prayer. As a disciple, *Extraordinary Christian Living* can be achieved when you incorporate those activities into your daily existence.

Evangelism is the reaching and saving of individuals through the sharing of one's belief about Jesus Christ.

This can be further explained through the messages of Elder Evelyn Murden and Ben Broadnax as they point out how church work can shape and provide momentum for Extraordinary Christian Living in the next section.

"I am a Praiser...I don't need anyone to encourage me to thank the Lord for what he has done for me!"
Evelyn Murden

Loyal Service
from Elder Evelyn E. Murden

"I'm totally loyal to the vision of the head of the Church."
Words of Wisdom from Evelyn E. Murden

Ordained Elder Evelyn Edwards Murden, The Singing Evangelist, promotes "notes of harmony" through being a loyal assistant to her pastor, her church, and through spreading God's Word through scripture and song. In a different time and place, she probably would have been an opera singer. Her voice is glorious and beautiful, and so is her heart. Born April 5, 1936, Elder Murden is full of vitality, grace, and affection for people.

Elder Murden Shares:

"I'm one of the Ordained Elders. There are 12 groups of us…Elders, Deacons, Missionaries, Women's Department, Men's Department, Children, Youth, Young Adults, Service, Outreach and more. I visit homes, I tend to all of the elderly—I have one lady who has dementia; I love her, and she ain't easy!"

"My church home is Holy Temple Cathedral, the headquarters for King's Apostle Church World Ministries, Inc. The organization is all over the United States, Africa, and it's big in Panama. 'My Bishop' (as she heartwarmingly calls him), is Prelate over the organization. This means that Pastor Bishop Wilbert Lewis Baltimore is the Senior Bishop and that all pastors, and all churches in the organization, are under him."

Ways I Serve during Service

"I'm involved as,

1. I go to speaking engagements with my pastor as minister— I'm very loyal, I support him, and I read the scriptures for him;

2. I'm with the choir;

3. I'm an exhorter, which means I encourage people to praise the Lord;

4. I'm an alter worker. When people come to the alter for prayer, if they have problems, they come up on the invitation to receive Christ. I also pray with them, give them scripture, and let them know that all the while they have Christ inside of them too;

5.   I occasionally direct worship services, as the Mistress of Ceremonies, we call it being a worship leader."

Ways I Serve Outside of Service

"I give service as,

1.   I share tapes and cd's from conferences I attend;

2.   I support the ministry in the vision of the Pastor. I'm totally loyal to the vision of the head of the Church (Jesus) and to Pastor, the under shepherd of the church. A minister needs someone like that, because there is no controversy and no static. While some people are dedicated, there may be people who have their own agendas/their own ideas about the ministry. There is a time and place for sharing, only when the floor is open. It's not proper to go to different people and talk negatively. We encourage people to go to the elders, not other members. Then, we will assist them, and take things to pastor, handling things in an orderly fashion. Elders have been promoted to do that."

Always on the go, she sees herself as a "junior senior"—taking care of those in need, while using her background as a geriatric nurse to train others to do the same.

"I know how to handle wheel chairs and patients. I have trained the deacons, men, and nurses at church in how to handle the invalid. When Mother Holiday became unable to walk, I trained the men how to lift her out of my car, in reverse. They would lift her and put her in the front pew with me. Then, one day, she got fresh! She loved it when the young men moved her. One day she said, "Murt, who is that young man? I don't know him?" …She would get a little extra strength when the young men came around!"

Lively, and oh so energetic, her voice is as lovely as an opera singer!

"I'm known for my hats, but when I became an Elder, I couldn't wear them with my ministerial attire. Though I love my hats, I love God and the opportunity to serve Him more! When they call me in for solos though, watch out! My gift is singing. I have sung on stage, off stage, on radio, and on TV. I've recorded with choirs several times. I was known as "the lady who could direct choirs" because people would wonder where those high notes were coming from since my back was to the public."

"Singing runs in our family!"

"My dad taught us piano, gave us voice and dance lessons. Once we were in his Cinderella production. My dad could sing, he was *way* ahead of his time with his voice. He played piano for his church in Philadelphia called Central Baptist Church on South Street, I think it's still there. In high school, I played the violin, and we would go to the Philadelphia Opera House."

"My mother could sing, and everyone in my nana's family could sing. And even today, my son has written over 500 songs and is singing music all over the country. I am blessed with two hard-working daughters who are mothers themselves; and I have four wonderful grandchildren. I'm proud of my little family. I'm grateful for who they are and for their contributions to my life and to the world. I appreciate what I learned as a child and I want people to listen to their children because they do have a voice."

"What I *Really* want people to know about God:

1. It pays for parents to take their children to church because that's where they learn about God and about Jesus Christ at an early age—learning in Sunday School. I learned the books of the Bible and how to find scriptures quickly, all because of the "Holy Young People's Union" program at my church. And even today, I read the scriptures for my Bishop. I can still find them quickly, before anyone else can.

2. When you grow up having gone to church, you learn the value of prayer and communication with God. Everyone has a gift(s). You can use your gifts. Being in a good Word church is a great place to find out what they are, and to use them in service to Him for the uplifting of people.

"Go to Church or Else!" said My Mother"
Ben Broadnax

Responsible Service
from Ben Broadnax

*"If God can save me or change me, there
is hope for any and everybody."*
Words of Wisdom from Ben Broadnax

**"Being an active church attendee has made a difference in
my life..."**

"That age old saying "An idle mind is a devil's workshop" is so true.
So my roots as a child in church and my mom's strict policy of 'if you
don't go to church, you don't go outside, you don't have company,
you don't play with games/toys, etc.' was in full effect...and Lord
knows, in those days I had to play with my GI Joe's."

"It keeps me grounded in knowing that church is where I am supposed
to be now, as an adult, and as a parent, I see and understand why."

"It helps me to raise my conscience about decisions I may face. As
a child in my neighborhood, we were brainwashed by friends who
stressed that only punks go to church; but, know that I'm grown, I
know that real men go to church."

Mr. Broadnax continues:
Three Practical Reasons People (and especially Parents) Should Attend Church

1. Folks that know me know my background, know my stories of growing up, and all the things I did or took part in. If God can save me or change me, there is hope for any and everybody.

2. If people have had a bad church experience, it's probably because they focused on a person rather than God. People can always disappoint or let you down.

3. Stories in the Bible help to give shape to my life, as well as that of many others. I believe the Bible is true, and the stories of the Bible come full circle in resembling stories in my own life.

Three Challenges Parents Will Face, If They Don't Share the Church Experience with Their Children:

1. According to my faith and the Word of God, if you don't know the Word, you won't know how to apply its principles. Consider Proverbs 22:6, *Train a child up in the way he/she shall go and when they are older, they will not depart from those ways.*

2. The Bible is a great book of instructions, and it gives us a great foundation for character building, lessons in humility, and teachings in how to treat one another.

3. In today's society, nothing else is working so, why not try Jesus?

Questions Asked of Mr. Broadnax:
What does working at the church mean to you?

"Just being on the premises to keep the "house in order" and to make sure that things are smooth, before, during and after worship, especially given some of the challenges and violence that has happened at churches throughout the years. Being able to offer expertise and assistance to secure the operations and to look for anything abnormal."

"I also get to interact and see the development of the children, who are at the daycare, and to have an impact of setting foundation for them."

"Working in the church is important. People are losing hope, that is, people who don't have any type of foundation. They seem to resist things that would provide a foundation and order, like church. Many have issues with church for one reason or another, and though it can't be explained, they lash out—although many churches seem to be doing really good work."

Ben Broadnax is Director of Security at Shalom Church, City of Peace, located in St. Louis, Missouri, where Dr. Freddy J. Clark is Pastor and Founder. An inspiring, Bible based message is always to be found at Shalom. If you find yourself in St. Louis on a Wednesday or Sunday, please stop by and see the wonderful things they are up to!

For more information, go to www.shalomchurch.org.

Chapter 12

Messages from Young Ministers

*"God is a field of inescapable, unalterable
eternal, and unconditional love."*
Reverend Kevin Ross

Things I Really Want Pioneering Church Leaders to Know...
The Reverend Kevin Kitrell Ross

Note to Readers from Jo Lena: This is an interview with Reverend
Kevin Kitrell Ross, Senior Minister and Spiritual Director of Christ
Unity Church, Sacramento, California. Reverend Ross is a friend of
mine. We met when he was a student at Morehouse College, and
I was studying to become a teacher through my home church in
Los Angeles, Understanding Principles for Better Living, which was
founded by Reverend Della Reese-Lett.

Kevin and I met on an "excursion" at the Crystal Cathedral (famed
church of Reverend Robert Schuler) while we were each accompanying
our "Spiritual Mothers"—mine, the late Rev. Delores F. McMillan,
known as Rev. Mac; and his, Dr. Johnnie Colemon). Our mentors
were great friends, and I appreciate that God worked it out so that
Kevin and I could meet under such favorable circumstances and also
become friends.

As we have each lived, faced challenges, grown, and matured since that time in 1996, we have supported each other in working toward understanding and fulfilling our life purposes. We have made efforts to keep each other informed and grounded when necessary. We have also had countless discussions about the responsibilities and requirements of church leaders and about meeting the needs of the younger generation, while benefiting from the lessons and wisdom of those who paved the way.

Having grown up at the church, Kevin was extremely clear about his path: he was planning to become an ordained minister. At a very young age, he was groomed to serve. He credits his most influential Spiritual Mentors as being Dr. Lawrence Edward Carter, Sr., Dean of the Chapel at Morehouse College; Father George Clements, Founder of One Church One Child; the Reverend Dr. Johnnie Coleman, Founder of Christ Universal Temple and the Universal Foundation for Better Living; the late Reverend Dr. Frederick Joseph Eikerenkoetter, II (better known as Reverend Ike), Founder of the United Christian Evangelistic Association; and the Reverend Dr. Michael Bernard Beckwith, Founder of Agape International Spiritual Center. I *really* wanted to know what Reverend Ross would say to church leaders of the "seasoned generation." Find below a few things he shared with me from our interview.

Reverend Kevin Ross Speaks:
Five Things I *Really* Want Pioneering Church Leaders to Know...

1. **That we thank you.** I want you to hear from our generation our gratitude for the foundation you have set and for the victories that you have won, that make it possible for us to have a platform.

2. **I'd like to bridge to you.** I like to create an intergenerational dialogue so that you will have a warm introduction into the world that is now, the newer traditions that are forming with the new generation. I want to bring you into the conversation. You, our forbearers—if only from us directly—we want you to know the current thinking, the current interpretations from this generation. This is a high-tech, low touch world. We don't have as much face-to-face contact as you used to have. Our tools are different. We want you to use those tools. Look at the internet; know how to use all the convenient features on the cell phone. We want to gently bridge for the mission, not force you. We aim to give you access now through to us to the new platforms.

3. **I want to include you.** We need and want the best of your wisdom as you take a new stance—going from center stage to a role of advisement and mentorship. We don't want to reject you; we still need you to take your place, which is one of honor. This is a stepping back place to observe and mentor; and, this is not a new conversation, from a Christian church perspective. We need to change some things so that we can make good choices and meet the needs of the people and their lives now. We need to hear from you, your foresight and hindsight, your advice that would assist us in gaining a foothold from a coach's perspective—but not by reprimanding us in public.

4. **I want to caution you.** There is danger in delaying succession because of fear that your legacy cannot be replicated, that no one else can do it or no one else is ready.

5. **I want to encourage you.** Know that it's going to be okay because, if for no other reason, we have a seed that you

have planted within us that will sprout in its due season. The right conditions will never be established if you forever remain center stage. Part of becoming an emerging leader is being able to rise up because he has the floor. If he never gets the floor, he won't have a shot or a clean slate. Let the back of the bicycle go and trust that the foundation you have laid can remain on its own.

Minister Kevin Ross says,

"My mission is to awaken each individual to live a life of purpose, passion, peace, and prosperity by teaching them distinctions for becoming what it takes to achieve what they were uniquely created to achieve. And, I do this through my coaching services, my retreats, my books, DVDs, and youth outreach."

Questions Asked of Reverend Ross:
Why is youth outreach important?

"Our world's youth are 100% of our future. And, when we invest in the emerging generation, we invest in the best of ourselves. We are only as strong as the weakest among us—and so far, in every society on earth, the weakest, the poorest, the most ignored, neglected, and abused are our world's youth—children."

So what if we keep down this path of ignoring them?

"My feeling is that, if we don't pay attention to them and focus on the critical concerns that face them right now, we set the stage for our own collective demise. There will be no regeneration, and we have to have regeneration for the system to work—for the human system to work."

Meet Reverend Kevin Ross and learn more at www.kevinrossspeaks.com.

Churchianity, God, and Chicken Dinners...
Pastor Cedric Portis, Sr.

"Because we are stewards of God, according to His Word, we
don't sell chicken dinners as fundraisers at our church."
Pastor Portis, Sr.

Note to Readers from Jo Lena Johnson: I knew of Cedric Portis because his younger brother was my co-worker at my first job—as a hostess at Ponderosa Steakhouse in 1986. Through the technology of Facebook, I recently noticed that Cedric Portis was now "Pastor Portis" and I contacted him to catch up. He told me about his ministry, and I was proud of his accomplishments and interested to see what this "young pastor" was up to.

Since this is a "21ˢᵗ Century Guide to Practicing Christian Living," I wanted to include this interview with him because his perspectives and practices offer food for thought, for the young and "the young at heart." This is for those of you who may be skeptics and don't think it's necessary to "rock the boat" and for those who want to "raise up to *extraordinary*" and are open to different viewpoints.

Cedric Portis was born in Mississippi in August of 1969. His parents moved the family to St. Louis when he was six years old. In 1980, their family started attending Third Presbyterian Church, where he remained until he got old enough to stop attending church without facing the wrath of his mom. He graduated in the Class of 1987 from Normandy High School and later from the University of Missouri-Rolla with a Bachelor's of Science in Mechanical Engineering in 1994. At Keller Graduate School of Management, he earned a Master's Degree in Project Management in 2000. Continuing his education, he graduated from St. Louis Christian College in 2002 with a Bachelor's Degree in Christian Ministry. Presently, he is attending the Eden Theological Seminary pursuing a Master's of Divinity.

In 1992, while a co-op student at Ameren UE (Union Electric), he met his wife Varonaki Portis who was also employed there. They married in 1994 and have one son, Cedric, Jr., who is currently in the 11th grade.

For years, although Cedric went to church and Bible study at the behest of his wife, he went on to teach Bible study for 72 weeks. During the time, he was practicing "Churchianity" (a phrase he coined; see meaning below). He says he put his Engineering Business first, then his DJ Business second, then God was third. Just as most of us, he had a "moment of clarity." One day he put aside the circumstances, which were between him and making God his #1 priority. He too, has a testimony. Cedric Portis went full-circle and returned to Third Presbyterian Church…in the capacity of "Pastor," where he has served for six years, since December 2003.

Pastor Portis has a lot he *really* wants people to know so, you will notice that I simply went with his answers and asked other questions. They are ones I felt that you, the reader, might also want to know.

Pastor Portis Shares:

"Churchianity," **means** that I understand and complete all the functionalities of being a church member but without living a Christian life. It means, "I have religion, but I don't have a relationship with Christ. Religion is what I "practice" in church, I stand, I sing, I pray when it's time or I'm told to do so. But, when I leave church, I leave Christ on the pew where I found Him. That's Churchianity."

Questions asked of Pastor Portis:
What do you want people to know about God?

"God loves you. You are his most precious creation. Know that you are never alone. Know that he protects you and calls you to be in a relationship with Him."

So, often times I feel alone, but you're telling me I'm not and never have been. So what can I do so that I'll know He's with me?

"You must learn of Him, and who He is. At church, people share what they've learned and seen—the evidence and activity of God. When you attend, you begin to "see" for yourself that He is real and active. You begin to have "proof" because you come to see what I see. You must learn about Him through the faith community because they give testimony to Him."

So in other words, you're telling me to come to church?

"Yes, that's where the faith community gathers for corporate worship of this living God. This is where you learn of Him."

I hear the word " testimony" a lot. What does that mean?

"This type of *testimony* is similar to the legal sense used in the courtroom, except that a person is testifying to a truth about their belief and faith in God. Testifying is sharing 'this is where I was, who I used to be, and how I've been changed' by this living God."

"God has provided a way for you to be redeemed. When man sinned, his relationship with God was fractured. So God enacted a plan of redemption to redeem man unto himself because the law of God states that the wages of sin is death. Sin is punishable by death; so therefore, death is required for man to be redeemed unto God. He loved you so much that he provided a way through the death of His Son Jesus. God awakens us or calls us…'those who respond to the calling of God are awake.'"

I'm not sure what you mean. Would you please explain further?

"I Corinthians 2:14 says, *But the natural man receiveth not the things of the Spirit of God: for they are foolishness unto him: neither can he know them, because they are spiritually discerned.* In other words, if you don't realize you are lost, you will not seek to be found. For example, if you were born on a desert island, that's what you would believe life to be. Therefore, if I don't see what it looks like to be saved, I think that what I see it normal because it is normal—but only for me."

"The law was meant to point us to a Savior…the Bible is a roadmap. You must know where you are to figure out where you are going. Once you realize that you don't know either where you are or where you are going, at least you know you are lost. You may come to realize that the Bible can show the way for you to go. If you don't get that from scripture, you made a wrong turn. Being in the Spirit allows for understanding, and God does that. He awakens people, through the Spirit, to Him."

> *"And not only so, but we also joy in God through our Lord Jesus Christ, by whom we have now received the atonement."*
> Romans 5:8

"He will judge sin; the wages of sin is death: that's the punishment. The good news is that those who have been redeemed do not face that judgment."

What is your ministry's mission?

"To provide for the physical and spiritual well-being of the congregation and surrounding community."

"Our church goal is that the ministry will be a resource provider to the community in which we reside. I can't get an audience with you spiritually until I meet you physically; nor can I make a difference in your life in some way that is tangible and real to you. For instance, if a person doesn't have a coat in the winter or they don't have food or a job, the physical needs that are real, tangible and pressing must be met. The needy can't "really" hear me until I meet them and help address those physical needs. Giving someone a dollar on the street is a waste of resources. I suggest saving those dollars and being intentional in someone's life. If I give someone $50 or $100 dollars, then I've gained audience with that person, and now the Gospel message may be able to take hold."

He continues,

What We Do at Third Presbyterian Church:

1. Vacation Bible Camp is a free summer program offered to youth who attend our church, and who are in our community. Every day from 8am to 4pm, the youth are cared for, nurtured and exposed to enriching activities. They are fed two meals daily in the process. Activities include praise dancing, learning theatre and dramatic acting, art, and field trips. It's all free.

    We inject this resource back into the community because, when we looked at our community, we felt that, *because we are here,* we want to make a difference. We are not here for business as usual. This community is full of young, single parent households where the parent must work. The household cannot necessarily afford $65–100 a week for camp, and we don't like the alternative—leaving the children unattended or supervised by siblings who are children themselves. That is a recipe for disaster. So, this is our big outreach effort. The first hundred that sign up get to attend, as we work through the Moline Acres City Government to spread the word.

2. We have a coat drive through which we clothe, with brand new coats, about 65 families a year—and most of the coats we purchase.

3. We host weekly Bible Study on Tuesdays. Afterward, we serve a fully cooked meal, feeding 100–150 people a week. We also have free nursery care any time the church is open. We do this so that all excuses are taken away, so people don't have to worry about anything but showing up to be fed physically and spiritually.

4. We have a back to school supplies drive each year in January, and we call it our "Finish Strong Campaign." Because after all of the drives that take place in August, by January all, the pens are broken and the backpacks are torn. We want the families to have the things they need to finish the semester strong because that's where the need is.

What We Don't Do at Third Presbyterian Church:

1. Because we are stewards of God, according to His Word, we don't do "chicken dinners" as fundraisers. We have been placed in the community to be edifiers and to build up

this community. I believe that resorting to "being in the restaurant business" even for a day is taking away profits from those who are in the restaurant business. It's not being good neighbors. It's like shaking a can on the street to get what you need.

And most people wouldn't "shake a can" in their personal life, and it won't happen at our church. We will never sell anything in this church to pay our bills. We rely on tithes and offerings; that's it. That's how we thrive because we are about more than surviving. This practice works very well at our church. We said to the congregation that we needed $10,000 for our floor at the church, and we needed it in 3 months. Our church is our home; so therefore, we looked at the sacrifices we could make so that God's house could have some new floors, and we got them.

2. We don't do a "Pastor's Anniversary" either. That practice comes out of the African-American church tradition. It started as an annual fundraiser for the pastor so that he could live above poverty. That was out of necessity, as was his coming over for Sunday dinner. It was because we did not have enough. It was wrong to do it then, and it is wrong to do it now. Why should we celebrate another year of the pastor being there? Don't worship me—I don't allow it because I don't have a heaven for you to go to. If you want to honor your pastor (me), come to Bible Study.

3. We don't keep people on the membership roster if we haven't had contact in over a year. Every November we make a membership purge to take people off. We set goals for growth every year, and we have probably grown about 200 members over the last 6 years since I've been Pastor. On

Sundays, we average 153 people a week and 115 in weekly Bible Study—and that's with a roll of 277 on the books.

Last question, I was told it was "impolite" to ask about membership numbers, yet you freely shared yours with me. Why?

Because being transparent is part of what I believe God would have us be.

Learn more about Reverend Cedric A. Portis Sr. and the ministry at www.thirdchurchstl.org.

SECTION FIVE: ACTION TO EXTRAORDINARY DAILY LIVING

Chapter 13

Figuring Out What You Really Want
Jo Lena Johnson

"People's behavior is, in reality, conditioned by habit, convention, deference, ignorance, and sometimes, downright irrationality."
William Alonso, American Economist

Your Journey and Quality of Life Depends on Your Roadmap!

In order to *be extraordinary*, just knowing something is not enough. Practice and experience make "skilled." Getting wisdom and understanding, along with discernment are Biblical. It's not enough to say, "I'm blessed and highly favored" without action. I do know that Jesus was "blessed and highly favored"…and so was Job. Yet, look at their life and experience! I urge you to have a "blessed and highly favored" attitude, along with "guided," orderly steps, and a plan of action.

144

It's not enough to say, "I'm going there" or "this is my goal." You must also know where you are, know where you intend to go, possess the tools, and know how to get there. While every person's life and experiences are unique, what we have in common is being spiritual beings in a human experience. By remaining connected to your source (God), you will have the ability to overcome any circumstances which you may find challenging.

Ultimately, if you rely on the human self—your own self or others— because you are not perfect, you will have challenges. This section is designed to guide you through your human condition, as you may have some specific factors interrupting your success.

> *"Blessed be the Lord, my rock, who trains my hands for war,*
> *and my fingers for battle; he is my steadfast love and my*
> *fortress, my stronghold and my deliverer, my shield; and he*
> *is whom I take refuge, who subdues people under me."*
> Psalm 144:1–2 (ESV)

"It's Your Choice! Choose a Destination and Thrive!"

What Do You Really Want? So many times people focus on what they don't want in life and forget about what they do want. Of course, in making a big purchase decision, such as a car, a home, or other real estate, we tend to take our time and do the research. We do so because we know a significant amount of money is on the line.

However, step back and think about other important areas of your life—your day to day thoughts, feelings, habits and practices. Are you satisfied and joyful, worried and afraid, or concerned and encouraged? Whatever your current state, your thoughts will dictate your new *extraordinary* results or keep you in the comfort or discomfort zone of whatever is normal for you.

"Let everything that has breath praise the Lord! Praise the Lord!"
Psalm 150:6

During victories and "mountain top" experiences when life seems to be going well, it's easy to "claim" what we did well. For example, "I got a raise," sounds *really* good, and it's not a hard thing to share, with the right people. However, saying, "I got a poor evaluation from my supervisor" may not be as easy to express. Telling somebody "negative things" about you or your life may not always be the easiest thing to state or share, or even acknowledge to yourself.

Your daily activities have the most impact on you, your family, and others who are in your life. My spiritual mentor, the late Reverend Delores McMillan would say to me, "Whatever you think about, you bring about;" and, depending on what topic we were discussing at the time, I had to *really* consider what I had done to cause the situation, circumstance, or challenge.

Another of Rev. McMillan's "favorite sayings to me" was "Leave it alone; leave it all the way alone!"

She would usually tell me this when we were discussing possible partnerships in business (I was working in Hollywood at the time) or in the area of relationships. I thank God that *our* relationship was one of trust, mutual love, and respect because through mistakes and successes, she made it safe enough to share. It's good to have people in your personal life that care enough to recognize who you are, love you in spite of yourself, and support you through your challenges or blind spots.

"When you make a mistake, there are only
three things you should ever do about it: admit
it, learn from it, and don't repeat it."
William Alonso

Great guidance and support can come from anyone, and often, younger people have plenty to say and share; however, they may hold back because their input has not necessarily been welcomed or appreciated in the past. Since we are talking about creating the *extraordinary*, I hope you will consider the value in "new." Innovation and flexibility are crucial to active, principled living in today's society.

In keeping with Rev. Mac's advice, young people have a way of communicating similar expressions but in slightly different ways. My cousin, Summer Knox, who is in her 20's, wrote a statement on her Facebook page, which I found rather profound: *"You can't be Superwoman if you keep kickin' it with Kryptonite. Make sure that the people you hang with make you stronger, not weaker."*

I would have never thought of it that way, or expressed it that way, yet there is a lot of depth to that statement. There are actually a lot of brilliant people in this world, including you. Still, if you don't make time to appreciate yourself, your priorities, and your effect on others, you may miss the opportunity to create extraordinary experiences.

Do you realize that you draw people to you every day?

You might have heard of "the law of attraction" or other similar principles found in new thought literature or in the best seller "The Secret." Your life, world, and affairs are what you make them. You model for yourself and others—and with clear vision, steadfast tenacity, resourcefulness, guidance, and God; you can have what you *really* want if you are willing to do the work.

Now, let's talk about other things that matter—relationships, communication, and personal responsibility. It's all about choosing healthy habits, routinely. Enjoying the people with and for whom you spend the most time loving, supporting, and providing. I urge you to look forward to opportunities to grow, expand, and to make new choices that will impact your life positively, if you chose to consider them.

When you know what you *really* want, and you are willing to research for input from experts, to actually take action, you can and will achieve your goals. One of the biggest challenges though, is when goals are not financial or tangible—when they are about those we love, quality of relationships, personal peace, satisfaction, and self-care, you know…work-life balance.

Days can be spent focused on earning money, saving money, investing money and spending money. They can be filled with meetings, schedules, routines, daily responsibilities, and old habits that die-hard.

In order to gain greater understanding, it takes clarity of purpose, flexibility, willingness, making good choices, and overcoming obstacles…

> *"Get rid of all bitterness, rage and anger, brawling and slander, along with every form of malice."*
> Ephesians 4:31

Defining Conflict

If you understand, you have the ability to apply. The number one cause of conflict is lack of (or) miscommunication. The primary cause of conflict, which is the lack of communication or miscommunication, is typically rooted in cultural differences.

Culture can include society, education, geographic territory, race, socio-economic class, or other factors. Yet, day to day, conflict between people most often happens for one of three reasons or all three reasons: Gender Differences, Generational Differences, or Personality Style Differences.

When you are attempting to accomplish a goal, it's important to know where you are going, why you are going, what tools you need, and how to actually use them; lest you forget the intended destination itself. Establishing routines and checks with balances along the way are crucial to *extraordinary living*. Notice it; the statement is not *extraordinary life*. Living is an action word. Everyday there are "opportunities" for conflict. Sometimes our conflicts are external; things like natural disasters; or they are internal like poor self-esteem or previous negative experiences; still, at other times they can be managed by your own willingness to learn, grow, stretch, and try different ways of thinking, acting, or behaving.

Extraordinary daily living isn't just about a big house, luxury cars, or fancy titles. Brilliance, powered through Spirit, glows wherever it grows. Overcoming conflict is addressed in the poem, *"Our Deepest Fear"*...

"Our Deepest Fear"

Our deepest fear is not that we are inadequate.
Our deepest fear is that we are powerful beyond measure.
It is our light, not our darkness that most frightens us.
We ask ourselves, Who am I to be brilliant,
gorgeous, talented, and fabulous?
Actually, who are you not to be?
You are a child of God.
Your playing small does not serve the world.
There is nothing enlightened about shrinking
so that other people won't feel insecure around you.
We are all meant to shine, as children do.

We were born to make manifest the glory of God that is within us.
It is not just in some of us; it is in everyone.
And as we let our own light shine, we unconsciously
give other people permission to do the same.
As we are liberated from our own fear,
our presence automatically liberates others.

Do you know who wrote "Our Deepest Fear?

A lot of people think it was Nelson Mandela. Considering that he spent more than two decades in a South African jail cell and then went on to become that nation's first Black President, wouldn't that be powerful? Can you imagine? Leaving jail and then delivering this speech at his Inauguration in 1994? Well, the above quote is often found on the internet credited, incorrectly, to Nelson Mandela, yet the author is Marianne Williamson, from her book, *"A Return To Love: Reflections on the Principles of A Course in Miracles,"* published by Harper Collins.

Now that you know who wrote the quote, it doesn't diminish the words, nor should it diminish the concept or the idea in your mind or experience. Yet, it's a great example of how miscommunication can happen. Somebody on the internet—with all of our wonderful technological advances, said "Nelson Mandela said it" and someone else ran off with the same information. Ms. Williamson is a prolific writer, and I'm a huge fan of her works. I also truly enjoyed reading the actual speech which Nelson Mandela delivered at his Inauguration. And, doesn't the whole episode lend itself to many life lessons about perspective, taking action, and context? They both have said something extraordinary. They have connected in thought and action with the same principle.

Your brilliance and your extraordinary life are your own. If you *really* want to experience it, you must find what liberates you and begin to embrace it.

How "Life" Impacts You

You learned a lot about life based on the behavior of your parents, your elders, your peers, your neighborhood, and other generational influences. Some things are easily modified and others, not so much. Choose to focus on what's most important to you. *The result?* What you *really* want—by knowing what you don't want!

Let's explore some basics, which will help you to overcome obstacles (conflict) while experiencing extraordinary living. Consider the definitions and reflections below.

TROUBLE—"Calamity, difficulty, disaster; the sure result of wrong thinking." All economic, social, and personal trouble can be traced back to selfishness of the "sense man." When "spiritual man" takes control of mind substance, all trouble of every kind dissolves into thin air. (From: *The Revealing Word: A Dictionary of Metaphysical Terms*, Unity Books, 1994)

It's easy to become so focused that the focus itself hinders progress. This has happened to me on several occasions. At the point when you realize that you are in the midst of the "cyclone," chaos, or overdrawn condition, it's time to stop and redirect your attention. Focus on God, as well as the life and teachings of Jesus Christ. Ask the Holy Spirit to work in your mind and heart to provide what you need in that moment. The Word of God is an excellent start.

Acts 16:31 says, *"Believe on the Lord Jesus Christ, and thou shall be saved."* As you explore reading the Bible, ask God to open your spiritual understanding so that the passages, which you require, will be so plain to you that it seems almost too simple!

DOUBT— *"Unsettled state of opinion concerning the reality of the truth of something"* (Webster). Doubt is the Satan of every man. Doubt is the root of weakness, mental and physical. If men had faith in themselves, in the ability of Spirit within them, they would become giants, where they are but pygmies. (Source: *The Revealing Word*)

FEAR—*"Painful emotion marked by alarm; dread; disquiet"* (Webster). Fear is one of the most subtle and destructive errors that the carnal mind in man experiences. Fear is a paralysis of mental action; it weakens both mind and body. Fear throws dust in our eyes and hides the mighty spiritual forces that are always with us. *Blessed are those who deny ignorance and fear and affirm the presence and power of Spirit.* (Source: *The Revealing Word*)

FEAR, how to overcome—Fear is cast out by perfect love. To know divine love is to be selfless, and to be selfless is to be without fear. The God-conscious person is filled with quietness and confidence. (Source: *The Revealing Word*)

This is your opportunity to *really* consider your priorities.

> *"You know how to overcome fear! Think about times when you "moved into action" and you didn't give it a second thought."*
> Ephesians 3:20–21 (NKJV)

Perspective Enables Extraordinary Christian Living!

Your perspective shapes your life, world, affairs, and choices.

What are you creating daily, in your life? Are you stuck in doubt or fear? Or, are you willing to sing a new tune or experience more of God through deeper awareness and connection to what you are thinking? How you are operating?

In coming chapters, you will be introduced to more people who have found the connections they needed to overcome conflict and achieve their extraordinary goals, and to make a difference in every life they touch. You, too, have that ability!

Chapter 14

Leadership: Establishing Your Priorities
Jo Lena Johnson

"I must really want to…"
Jo Lena Johnson

*"Wisdom is the principle thing; therefore get wisdom:
and with all thy getting, get understanding!"*
Proverbs 4:7

There are five main areas of life which are concerns for most people—meaning that the things that are priorities in most of our lives can usually be grouped into the categories. I've found the "grouping" to be a pretty good approach to focusing on what's important, what's not important, and the opportunities for growth and development.

Jo Lena Johnson Shares:

The Five Main Areas of Extraordinary Living

1. Health;

2. Work/Education;

3. Relationships/Family;

4. Finances; and

5. Spirituality/Community.

You can use these categories to determine what you do want versus what you don't want when choosing your priorities. Each of us, at times, has given space to things like stress, tension, poor health, frustration, poverty, or any other challenges you may be facing now.

What do you really want? For you? For your life? For your family? For your future? And, what are you willing to do in order to get there? Sometimes, it's a matter of just knowing where to start, and, of course, how to finish!

> *"I Ain't Never Been Nothing but a Winner"*
> Paul "Bear" Bryant

Communicating

Since we are human, we can only share with you things according to our understanding. Yet, there is a place where you can get ALL of the answers and instruction you need, in and through reading and understanding the Word of God through my favorite book, the Holy Bible.

Yet, interpreting the Bible in a way that makes sense to you is a spiritual mission; a personal, private, exceptional, and *extraordinary* journey to and through yourself. I suggest that you ask God, even in this very moment, to lead you to the lessons that you need, according to your own unique purpose and circumstances.

> *"Be completely humble and gentle; be patient,*
> *bearing with one another in love."*
> Ephesians 4:2

Go to God and ask Him for what you need, He will direct you—and He might also bring people into your life to demonstrate what you need to see, know, and understand. I believe that happens to me on a daily basis.

Yet, confusion and conflict can happen over some of the smallest, seemingly normal things. The principles below will help you along your journey:

If You Understand, You Have the Ability to Apply.

PROVERB—A short, pithy statement about the nature of man and life.

In the Bible, Solomon is singled out for his use of proverbs. I Kings 4:32 says, *"And he spake three thousand proverbs: and his songs were a thousand five."* Solomon's wisdom was shown by his ability to make clear, true commentaries upon the nature of things. The Hebrew word most frequently translated as proverb means literally "a similitude," or loosely, "a representation." *So when God declared that Israel would be "a proverb...among all peoples"* (1 Kings 9:7), He implied that the name "Israel" would come to symbolize disobedience.

Proverbs are designed to make God's truth accessible to all people, so they might direct their lives in accordance with His will. (Source: *Nelson's Bible Dictionary*)

Now that you have a definition of a Proverb, does it help you? Does it make you want to just dive into the Bible and say; I want to learn a pithy statement about man and life? Probably not. However, the purpose of the Proverbs is to help us to *live extraordinarily*, if we are willing to *really* try. Most people have at least heard about King Solomon, David's son, King of Israel. The first seven verses of the Book of Proverbs share its purpose—or clear intent.

The Purpose of Proverbs
These are the proverbs of Solomon, David's son, King of Israel.

Their purpose is to teach people wisdom and discipline,
to help them understand the insights of the wise.
Their purpose is to teach people to live disciplined and successful lives,
to help them do what is right, just, and fair.
These proverbs will give insight to the simple,
knowledge, and discernment to the young.

Let the wise listen to these proverbs and become even wiser.
Let those with understanding receive guidance
by exploring the meaning in these proverbs and parables,
the words of the wise and their riddles.

Fear of the LORD is the foundation of true knowledge,
but fools despise wisdom and discipline.
Proverbs 1:1–7 (NLT)

Those words are straight from the Bible. You now have a choice, even if you have never seen them before; you now know where you can find answers when you need them. Choose a Proverb a day to ponder. You have so much to gain that what could you possibly have to lose?

Living as a Leader:
Questions and Considerations

- *Do you know what you really want?*

- *Can you share that vision with yourself and others in a way that they "get it"? In a way, that's clear to you and anyone else who is affected by the vision?*

- *Are you willing to focus single-mindedly on purpose driven good works, whatever the method, channel, or opportunity for growth even when challenging?*

- *Do you show yourself and others respect by being personable, articulate, trustworthy, and appreciative of the differences— even when you don't want to be or it doesn't feel good?*

- *Are you serious enough to study, and to listen to sound wisdom? Are you willing to seek out guidance and to question what's easy to see, and what may be missing?*

- *Are you courageous enough to stand up for your own morals, values, judgments, standards and for those of others who may not know, be able to, may not understand, or who simply may not care?*

- *Are you in touch with your primary resources? Your thoughts, time, talent, and feelings are those precious resources that, once dwindled, are very difficult for you to restore by yourself.*

- *What are the areas that get the most attention from you? What are the areas wherein lie the most opportunity for growth?*

In my leadership classes, I ask these questions and more… When you think about the five primary areas of concern for your life, begin to consider what you are doing to contribute to or to take away from the things that are most important to you. What are the ones you really care about?

The reality is, most managers and supervisors—across the board in terms of industry, have not had leadership training. To actively practice Christian Living, it takes courage, awareness, and overcoming considerations.

Whether you are a young adult, seasoned adult, or somewhere in between, what you do and say; don't do and say; and what you show makes a difference.

7 Leadership Activities from Jo Lena Johnson

1. Put God first.

2. Show the posture of a servant: turn humility and confidence into tenacity, especially when times are tough.

3. Forgive yourself and others; no one is perfect, and especially not you!

4. Build and maintain relationships with people who look like you and who don't look like you; it's critical to your success.

5. Be willing to let go of those situations, circumstances, and people who no longer deserve you.

6. Be willing to admit when you don't know need to know and when you don't understand.

7. Be willing to *be* in action and in living. *Be extraordinary in your living because you really want to*—and because you are willing to practice, be precise, and be wise!

Chapter 15

Legacy: Establishing Your Lasting Value
Jo Lena Johnson and Wise Friends

"It might be really tough."
Jo Lena Johnson

"But speaking the truth in love, may grow up into him
in all things, which is the head, even Christ."
Ephesians 4:15

Your behavior affects so many people and that's why leadership "standards" are important to establish. Since I've given you a lot of questions, I also want you to have some specifics to consider so that you can make some well-informed, substantial choices to take you from where you are to where you really want to be.

Consider these topics:

A. Health: Food, exercise, habits. What are you taking in? What are you doing? What are you giving up?

B. Finances: Earnings, debt, savings. Where are you earning your money? What debts do you have? Which do you *really* need? Do you understand the power of compound interest? Have you established and continued to maintain savings? Are you prepared for times of crisis?

C. Community: Who are those being served by you, and why? What difference are you making? What is your legacy?

D. Spirituality: Whom are you serving? What difference are you making for you? For others in the universe?

E. Work(s)/Career:

    1. What is the end goal?

    2. What are you producing?

    3. Why are you even here?

    4. What will it take for you to focus and earn the right to be listened to and trusted?

    5. In your Performance and Professional Development, what are you contributing?
        Are you …
        a. Studying?
        b. Learning?
        c. Broadening your scope?
        d. Cutting out the nonsense?

F. Education: Are you open to learning? Are you engaging others and asking tough questions? Are you rising above to your own standards? Are you investing the time and making education a priority for yourself and for those around you?

G. Relationships/Family: Where is your grounding? In what way are you "showing yourself approved?" Are you open to communicating across generational lines—and to understanding and relating to others' points of view? Are you *really* committed to living life extraordinarily, or are you super comfortable with status quo or mediocrity? Do you know what language you and your loved ones speak? And what are you doing to master it?

Building on the Shoulders of Others

Do you seek guidance among those who are exemplifying *Extraordinary Leadership/Living?*

Have you considered your own Legacy?

In this chapter, you will meet accomplished persons in the area of their disciplines and vocations. They have some things they really want to share with you.

As you are on your path to creating your Extraordinary Legacy, please keep the Leadership Questions from Chapter 14 and the Legacy questions from this chapter close at hand…and yes, "It might be really tough…" That's why this is called "If you really want to…"

Creating Legacies through Your Song (Psalms)

What's your song?

Please think about it. If you were to name your top three all time favorite songs?

With your primary thoughts, the ones you have daily, you are creating your own psalms. The Bible tells us that King Solomon was responsible for "one thousand five" psalms. How powerful. God used him to share with us some good wisdom, praise, expression, and comfort—timeless generational gifts available for us in our moments of need. At most, of the funerals I've attended, the 23rd Psalm has been presented as a source of strength and solace. What has your experience been with Psalms?…And what is a psalm?

PSALM—The Truth of God spoken in poetry or music; a hymn of praise or joy; spiritual aspiration of the soul. *"Is any cheerful?" Let him sing praise."* James 5:13 (Source: The Revealing Word)

God has an open invitation for you and me. He also gives us the ability to "in-joy" Him through our very own psalms (songs). If a tape recorder were to start right now and record every thought you have about yourself, your life, and those who populate your space for a twenty-four hour period, would the recording be a hit or a miss? Would your thoughts create songs of trouble, fear, or doubt?

Lyrics are powerful, and they produce results.

What you and your family *replay* daily affects your life, your mission, and your outcome.

As previously mentioned, Dr. Edwin Bailey, Jr. mentioned his two favorite songs. It's interesting because one of them, "I Won't Complain," was greatly popularized by a young preacher, Reverend Paul Jones. He was 30 years old at the time that he recorded this particular version. As you read the lyrics, please think and compare them to your most frequent thoughts about your life, circumstances, and outlook. When you are willing to "be cheerful" and "sing praises," you allow the Truth of God to fill you up. You reject those thoughts and feelings that are part of the "worn out recordings."

Please don't just skim over the words below because you "think you know them" or "it's easier." Allow them to sink in—please!

"I Won't Complain"
Version as recorded by the Reverend Paul Jones

[Verse 1:]
I've had some good days, I've had some hills to climb.
I've had some weary days. And some sleepless nights.
But when I look around, and I think things over,

All of my good days, Out-weigh my bad days; I won't complain.

[Verse 2:]
Sometimes the clouds are low, I can hardly see the road.
I ask a question, Lord, Lord, why so much pain?
But he knows what's best for me; Although my weary eyes they
can't see.

So I'll just say thank you, Lord. I won't complain.

[Chorus:]
The Lord Has been so good to me.
He's been good to me; More than this old world or you could ever
be;
He's been so good, To me; He dried all of my tears away;
Turned my midnights into day; So I'll just say thank you, Lord.

[Ad-lib:]
I've been lied on. But thank you, Lord.
I've been talked about. But thank you, Lord.
I've been misunderstood. But thank you, Lord.
You might be sick; Body reeking with pain. But thank you, Lord.
The bills are due; Don't know where the money coming from;
But thank you, Lord. Thank you, Lord. Thank you, Lord.

[Chorus:]
I want to thank God. Has been so good to me. He's been good to
me.
More than this old world or you could ever be.
He's been so good. He's been so good. He's been so good.

So good. So good. So good. So good. To me.
He dried all of my tears away; Turned my midnight into day.

[Ending:]
So I'll just say thank you, Lord, I won't complain.

[Source: *"I Won't Complain," Lyrics on http://www.lyricsmania.com/*]

Dr. Jefferson talked to us about "Order" in his "Seven Keys" earlier
in the book. Part of being orderly is answering your "calls" when
they come. Have you ever put off something you knew you were
supposed to do or even felt the strong urge to do, and you didn't do
it? Well, we learned that extraordinary living is about being urgent
and precise. We cannot afford to have you delay in finding or living
your purpose. Perhaps something you are deemed and destined to
do will bring comfort, inspiration, help or healing to millions, much
like the song "I Won't Complain" probably has for you or many.
There is more to this song than "meets the eye…"

> *Rev. Paul Jones (1960–1990) was the founding Pastor*
> *of New Grove Missionary Baptist Church in Houston,*
> *TX. Rev. Jones was a dynamic preacher and singer*
> *whose life was cut short at the youthful age of 30 when*
> *he was murdered at his home in the Houston area in*
> *1990.*
>
> [Source: *The Black ChurchExperience.blogspot.com*]

Talk about *extraordinary!* The follow-up story goes deeper:

> *In summary, Rev Jones was at home (Houston area) late one Sunday night around midnight when two men knocked at the door. Supposedly, he knew one of them (a 19 yr-old male). They forced their way in, shot him three times in the back, buttocks and back of head. He was robbed, and his car was stolen.*
>
> *For the record, he did not write "I Won't Complain." He recorded his version of the song in 1990. Actually the night of his murder, it was recorded. The original author is Bishop William C Abney. Savoy records released "The Rev Paul Jones CD" posthumously...he was 30 years old at the time of his murder. God Bless.*
> [Source: *Onestopfaqs.com*]

Did you notice what the note said? "I Won't Complain" was recorded the night of his murder. In 2003, a young man pleaded guilty and was sentenced to 20 years for aggravated robbery.

In 30 short-lived years, Reverend Paul Jones created a lasting legacy. Think about your age and your lyrics. What is your song? Extraordinary living is about experiencing your life's purpose so clearly that the rest of us naturally benefit as a result of your life and works.

If you have been unclear in your purpose, perhaps this sad, yet inspiring, story of a young man, who was meant to comfort millions with his legacy, will help you to see that pushing forward is a great start for you.

Let's Circle Back—What's your Song?

If every time you had a problem or a challenge and you listened to words found in Psalms, imagine how inspired you might be to keep pushing on and through to your extraordinary life results.

Remember what Reverend Mac said, "Whatever you think about, you bring about!"

It doesn't mean ignore the problems or challenges, or act like they aren't bothering you. It's a matter of allowing His Spirit to show you what to do, and how to do it. If you pick up your Bible and open it to the Book of Psalms, there is likely one that will address your needs. Living an *Extraordinary Christian Life* is not about "acting as if" it's about acknowledging and allowing God to be active in your life through living.

> *"I will sing of steadfast love and justice; to*
> *you, O Lord, I will make music."*
> Psalm 101:1 (ESV)

Establishing Legacies (Health/Service)

"My experience taught me that Acupuncture, along with making some changes in my diet, could help to restore my health—and the needles didn't hurt!"
—Jo Lena Johnson

Fitness and Good Health
Afua Bromley, L.Ac—St. Louis Acupuncture

Note from Jo Lena Johnson: *What are you currently digesting? Good Health is imperative. Due to poor choices, too many people are killing themselves because of food and vanity. It's important to consider alternatives to what you are doing, if it's not really working for you. I know this through experience. I've struggled with my weight most of my life. And, being on the road, traveling from city to city, sometimes five days a week to five different cities can wreak havoc on the body. I know because I've lived it. I actually lost my voice for a couple of months in the beginning of 2009. It was a time of professional and personal transition for me, and I believe it was a miracle and blessing—now, I can say that.*

My body was literally breaking down. Problems that I never dreamed of having started occurring. Even my knees began to bother me, not when I was standing up, but when I was sitting down! I went the "traditional medicine route," but nothing seemed to work; so I prayed harder, listened more, and went to an Acupuncturist. The treatments helped me. Yet, to truly be healthy, it was going to take changes in sleeping patterns, diet, a reduction in stress, worry, and fear—and an increase in Faith, healthy habits, and rest.

If you have never considered Acupuncture, or if you have, the following interview with Afua Bromley, L.Ac is full of great insight for healthy living. Pay special attention to the section about diet foods and such. It's extremely helpful and will make a difference for you and your family... if you are willing.

Afua Bromley, L.Ac (Licensed Acupuncturist) Shares

"Being a Licensed Acupuncturist has been what I thought it would be. One of the things I really like is that I have a wide variety of people; so I am never bored. And, too, I'm able to use all of the tools that I learned in school to help people and also to help people help themselves. I'm constantly challenged. I also like the fact that I can help people take better charge of their health."

Afua Bromley Shares:
Six ways to stay out of an Acupuncturist's or Doctor's Office (or at least minimize your time spent there)... Takes Healthy Practices!

1. Get enough sleep.

2. Stretch and exercise regularly—with a big emphasis on stretching.

3. Take time to reflect, whether it is meditating or praying; however, people need to reflect.

4. Have at least 60% of what you eat be vegetables and fruit (at a minimum).

5. Drink at least 64 ounces of water a day (for an adult).

6. Give or get a hug at least once a day.

Questions Asked of Afua Bromley:
Why this list?

"For the most part, it covers a lot of mental health issues. Following this regiment helps to deal with stress and manage mental health issues, such as depression. I see a lot of both. And, because I truly care, I actually want people to get better. Sooner than later, I hope that I don't have to see you at my office, but maybe I'll see you out and about."

"I had a patient who was complaining of knee problems, among other issues, and I recommended that she practically eliminate both salt AND sugar from her diet *(this case may sound familiar to you, Jo Lena, as she says with a smile).*"

"I recommended eliminating salt because she was retaining fluids; and sugar because it tends to have an inflammatory effect on the body, especially with joints."

"I also recommended that she stop drinking all of the diet caffeinated soda that she was using to stay awake instead of sleeping."

Reasons to Eliminate Certain Drinks (and "diet" foods):

1. **Carbonated Beverages:** Any time you are drinking them, it's tough on the kidneys. You usually run an increased chance of developing kidney stones because it's a mineral; so even when drinking seltzer water with no calories, it's harder for the kidneys to process.

2. **"The Diet Part":** In any kind of diet products, there is the whole element of chemical additives. Some of the artificial sweeteners are known to increase your cancer risk,

like saccharine. Others are reported to increase the risk of developing auto immune diseases and memory issues—with an increased risk of developing Alzheimer's and Dementia. And, though some of those studies are controversial, I don't think it's worth taking the chance.

There are more recent studies showing that, generally speaking, people who drink diet sodas are usually still shown to remain overweight. They actually think there is some evidence that the body doesn't process the artificial sweetener like a non-calorie. You don't usually see a whole bunch of people who are overweight lose weight by drinking them…and people who are thin and drink them usually stay thin.

Does Acupuncture hurt?

"It doesn't hurt, most of the time—you can fit five acupuncture needles into a syringe. Techniques do vary from one practitioner to another."

How does water intake play into acupuncture?

"When you are dehydrated, the needles don't go smoothly into the skin—there is more resistance in the muscle and in the skin. So drinking water creates a better environment and a more relaxing experience."

What if I'm afraid of needles?

"Go in; ask the acupuncturist to do just one needle. After you get one, you will probably say, "Wow! That's it?" and then you will be ready for a full treatment. It doesn't hurt, and, after the first one needle, sometimes you don't even know that more are being placed."

Is acupuncture expensive?

"It's not costly. It is sometimes covered by insurance; so, it behooves you to find out. If you go into someone's private practice, office visits will vary anywhere from $45 to $95; however, if that is out of your price range, there are other options:

1. Go to an Acupuncture School where you will be seen by a student who is supervised by a licensed practitioner. Those visits are usually $25.

2. Go to a community Acupuncture Clinic, which often runs on sliding scales. There the treatment can cost from $15–20 up to about $45.

Some of the other services I offer are quite helpful to people—and I really enjoy teaching them how to take care of themselves."

I Do Food Therapy.

"This is what I call food and dietary energetic medicine. When people find out about it, they get excited because they realize that, 'If I get this particular food I will have this particular result.' For example, I recommended pears to a patient who came in with a raw sore throat because they help to soothe the throat immediately. It's so simple and it works. It gets rid of your sore throat."

I Do "Cupping."

"Cupping creates suction using a glass jar, and it works on the deeper layers of muscle tissue to loosen them. Particularly for neck and back pain, it helps the body heal more quickly."

"If you have a friend, spouse, or relative, once or twice a week, you can use this tool at home to relieve your muscles."

"I like to share these things because people get better and actually refer others to me. The whole point is they are better and getting better quicker."

I also show people different acupressure points.

"By knowing where their acupressure points are located, people can work on their root issues. While they may be feeling ill, this may be a temporary fix—but relief, nonetheless."

"For example, I do acupuncture labor induction, which means that I actually stimulate women to go into labor. One of my patients was overdue and her contractions were starting. I showed her how to find the acupuncture points, so she could continue to press the points to stimulate the contractions and show her husband where they are. He then could help speed it along as well."

What's the big project in Ghana you are building?

"I am the Director of a non-profit that has an HIV women's support group, along with HIV prevention in St. Louis. I'm also helping to build an integrative medicine non-profit clinic in Ghana, West Africa."

Why is this clinic so important?

"It is a pilot/model which will hopefully be reproduced worldwide… the idea is that integrative medicine can address the various health care needs of different people. It has a strong emphasis on training public health care workers above and beyond the norms."

What does integrative medicine mean?

A wide variety of different modalities (health care practices).
- a. Acupuncture
- b. Traditional herbal, local medicines
- c. Counseling
- d. A "Western Medicine MD"
- e. A Midwife
- f. Possibly a Homeopath or another health care field

Wow, how do you find the time to do this?

"I'm a workaholic."

"We have the land and a water source, and we are in the process of building the facility. In terms of health care in Ghana, in the semi-rural areas, there is limited access. Nationally, in Ghana there is one health care provider per 10,000 people, so access is an issue."

Afua Bromley is up to *Extraordinary Living*, and she is empowering others to do the same.

If you want to learn more about the project in Ghana, or to support it, please visit Universalhealth.net.

If you are ready to learn more about Acupuncture or to schedule an appointment, go to www.acupuncturestlouis.com for more.

Establishing Vision (Education/Work)
*"There was no Plan B for me when I was pursuing my
dream—it meant that I was going forward, regardless."*
Dr. Candace Wakefield

Creating the *"Children's Dental Zone"*
Dr. Candace Wakefield, D.M.D.

Committed, bright and extremely well educated, Dr. Wakefield. We *really* wanted to know the real reasons "Dr. Candy" chose Pediatric Dentistry; and just like her, the answers are delightful! She shows us that vision, technical ability, and training can be incorporated into providing invaluable services with purpose and fun, all rolled into a lucrative and successful practice.

Dr. Wakefield spent 4 years working in a research lab while gaining her BA in Biological Sciences at the University of Missouri-Columbia. She then attended Southern Illinois University School of Dental Medicine and graduated in May 2000 with a D.M.D. (Doctor of Dental Medicine). Dr. Wakefield was prepared, engaged and educated, ready to succeed in her dental practice. She didn't stop there! She obtained a Certificate in Pediatric Dentistry in May 2002 from Howard University.

In September 2005 she became board certified in Pediatric Dentistry. This was an optional certification (in dentistry) it's the icing on the cake. At the time of her receiving the certification, she was the only female board certified pediatric dentist in the State of Missouri.

Dr. Candace Wakefield Shares Why She Created Her Business
The Children's Dental Zone:

1. I enjoy working with children—it allows me to be who I am. My personality is best suited for working with children because I am a "happy go lucky," carefree individual. I like to laugh, and I feel most comfortable in that setting. I like music, cartoons, and the excitement level of it all. And, during my training, that's where my niche happened to be and where I seemed to excel the most. It was my natural gravitation.

2. Everything I do is centered on having fun. I knew my legacy was dentistry and working with children is where it all fit.

3. I like working with my hands, and I like creating things. With the small areas and actually aiding things, conditions, I consider myself to be a little of an artist.

   I realized while studying during the preparatory course for the Dental Aptitude Test that I excelled in the perceptual ability portion of the test. It's where you learn upside down—about shapes and looking at things from different angles—and you state options about what you can do with them. Objects were shaped a certain way, similar to origami on paper...nothing I had never seen before. It appealed to the artist in me. I took the test, passed it, got accepted to dental school, and the rest is history.

4. Becoming a Pediatric Dentist was the best decision I ever made in my life, and that was that.

Five Steps to Vision and Success from Dr. Candace Wakefield

1. Believe in God. He knows what's in your future; put your trust and faith in Him, and let Him guide you.

    Never let someone tell you what you can't do. I ran into that with counselors and deans in my career. Never let someone talk you out of your own potential.

2. Always invest in your education. It's what will take care of you, and it will pay for itself in the end. Don't be afraid to pursue it because of costs. The value will be well-worth it.

3. If there is something you really believe in, stick with it. There was no Plan B for me when I was pursuing my dream. The pursuit meant that I was going forward, regardless.

    Even when it gets hard and difficult and dentistry is not for the faint of heart, things are going to happen. Then you have to step up your game and improve. You can't float and let things pass by. You must continually pursue your vision, your dreams; and you must stay abreast of changes. Technology does not stop once you get out of school.

4. If you want to get the best job, you have to compete to become the best. Constantly prepare yourself. Education is always changing, like sports and technology.

5. To Parents: **Support your child** in endeavors, and be a good example, even if you didn't have good examples growing up.

    If you don't know how to be a good example, find someone who can be. Put someone in your child's life or find someone or something that has a needed someone there. Find programs, examples of aspiration for your child so there can be role models, so they don't get lost in the cracks, so they can have hope for the future that is better than your own.

Support the education and opportunities for your child, which include home training, education, and spiritual nurturing—those are the fundamentals.

Meet "Dr. Candy" at www.thechildrensdentalzone.com or www. facebook/thechildrensdentalzone.com.

Establishing Legacies (Family/Work)
"You have the power to do whatever you want in life—it is within you."
Zachary Hawkins

From Dallas to Wall Street
Zachary K. Hawkins

Zachary Hawkins was born and raised in Dallas, Texas, on December 26, 1964. He grew up with his brothers Jeff and Tony, and they were raised by their single mother, Joyce Hawkins. He graduated from South Oak Cliff High School and then earned a Bachelor Degree in Business Administration from the University of North Texas at Denton, where he pledged Alpha Phi Alpha, Fraternity, Incorporated in the Spring of 1984.

Zachary is husband to Karen Hawkins and father to Zachary Austin Hawkins, age twelve; and Zion Alexander, age nine. Zachary's eldest is Jazmine Hawkins, a college student in Dallas. Zachary Hawkins is the Executive Director and Head of Business Development of Treasury Services for JP Morgan.

Mr. Hawkins defines leadership as, "Being able to get people aligned to a vision; being able to help motivate them; and helping them to execute and achieve the vision. It means a lot in different situations, such as helping them determine where they are trying to go and helping them actually get there. It takes on different forms." He says he learned that through his personal experience.

Zachary Hawkins' Five Daily "Must Do's" List:

1. **Meeting my responsibilities by getting up and being productive each day.** This means making good use of my time, getting some type of return financially, and, ensuring that my family has their needs met.

2. **Taking care of my personal hygiene and health.** You are the engine; otherwise, there is no ability for you to meet your commitments to be healthy and "fresh."

3. **Stay sharp and read.** Getting information that will enable you to be more effective, as research and knowledge help you to be wise.

4. **Be reflective and think about what is going on in life.** Think about "the past," "your present," and the next steps to move yourself forward. Times of introspection are important. You can't always run around without taking time to think. Include God, talking to Him in mediation and in prayer. Also, spending time listening is crucial. He plays a major role in my life.

5. **Cultivate relationships.** Building equity with family, and with business acquaintances who are all part of the team in which I am engaged.

Statistics say you shouldn't have made it this far. What happened?

"In my particular case, continuously getting out of my comfort zone has helped me. My life was based in a 15-mile radius of Dallas, going away to college and then leaving Texas helped me to stretch and grow. I left the telecom industry to go to the pharmaceutical industry in Philadelphia. I went from sales to marketing to new product development, dealing with existing business, then US business, into the Global market, and then Wall Street."

"Many of the roles I took on were not things I had done before. My willingness to do things that would put me in an uncomfortable position, that's part of the secret to my success."

"Doing things that are outside your comfort zone and challenging yourself are necessary; and they work. That has been a driving force in my success. It's critical for me. It also means getting in front of people to deliver presentations. I wasn't very good at it in the beginning, and then I started doing better. All along the way, I was building credentials."

Six Steps to Extraordinary Achievement in the Workplace from Zachary Hawkins:

1. **Learn to be a good problem solver.** Problem solving is how you work through the appropriate solutions and evaluate options. Engage others to assist you or give you guidance and input, when needed.

2. **Define the right problem.** Identify what the real problem is and this includes going beyond the workplace by relating to your own personal welfare, health, and family and by figuring out what will be the best course of action after that.

3. **Keep your poise.** Remain grounded in all scenarios. Being "emotionally unfit" drives a lot of our actions, thoughts and choices. Don't allow circumstances to beat you down; respond in a way that will allow you to get through versus cracking, crumbling or blowing up.

4. **Build a support system.** Align yourself with the right people, and insure they are really with you when things get tough.

5. **Know your true self.** You have to really understand who you are—your tendencies, your strengths, your weaknesses and how you react in different situations. Know your habits and be able to step outside of yourself; be able to shift when you need to. Do not marry things outside your principles.

   Know what your strengths are and leverage them to open doors for you. Don't underestimate the value of developing your soft skills. They can take you places you cannot imagine. You can leverage them to be as successful as the hardcore functional type skills.

6. **God.** Spirituality is always important. It's not just what you can see while being able to be successful and reach your potential. You may function everyday, personally and professionally—but then there is a spiritual aspect that defies logic.

   Being prayerful, optimistic and regularly reading Scripture allow you to stay connected, tap into the Source, and lean on God. That's important. You *must* have faith beyond the things you can actually see. If you have that force on your side, you can reach your *extraordinary you.*

Remember: Preparation plays a huge role in success. It includes discipline—everything we do in our lives. The intentional or unintentional equips us to do our best. It can be motherhood, fatherhood or a job. They all play a major role, but we must put the work in to be extraordinary.

Mr. Hawkins is writing a book—From Statistic to Success - Five Fundamentals Mothers Must Master When Raising Boys Alone. This book is to provide single moms with the parenting skills to help them raise good sons.

Establishing Legacies (Community)
*"You must believe in yourself—then you
will be able to believe in others."*
Martin Luther Mathews

Martin Luther Mathews
Team, Works

Martin Luther Mathews is a legend. His life's work has been to empower young people to their greatness through providing an outlet for sports, activity, skill building, structure, expression, safety, engagement, and plain old love. Respected, admired, and focused, over one million lives have been impacted by Mr. Mathews and his band of visionaries. As such, they have been individuals willing to do the work, put in the time, and donate to sustain the 50-year-old *Mathews-Dickey Boys' & Girls' Club that he founded in St. Louis, Missouri.

Mr. Mathews Shares:
Three Things, Which Will Carry You through Anything in Life
1. Credibility
2. Integrity
3. Accountability

Mr. Mathews says,

"In America, we have one of the greatest countries in the world. You must use resources and gain the confidence in people who believe in you to help you reach your goal in life. Use resources that are available to you. Try to get someone to help those that you really want to help."

"In America, if you read the Constitution and Bible, it is implied, if you work hard at something, you will achieve it. This should be a goal not only for ourselves as individuals, but also for the people, we serve. By following the principles found in these documents, you will make a better place for yourself and for humanity."

"We started out with nothing, but, in many ways, we had the dream that Christopher Columbus had. We had a dream of a better life, not only for ourselves but for those we serve."

Questions Asked of Mr. Mathews:
How did Mathews-Dickey start?

"There is something that people never know for sure—where the world will take you. A.C. Anderson was a man in the community who was concerned about the young men and wanted help."

"We met in his dining room one day because he wanted to do something, but didn't have the means and the necessary connections.

So, he summoned me. I was able to take the tools I learned in my lifetime and share them with the 30 boys he introduced to me. In that group of young men, nearly 100% went on to be successful in achieving their goals in life."

"Can you share with us a story of how helping one of these young men jump-started your legacy?"

"A young man named Taylor Fields is a great example. He was one of my '10 Top Challenges,' as I like to call him. He graduated high school in January, only a year after his brother had graduated. Their parents were able to get his brother off to college, but they weren't prepared to send Taylor. He got acquainted with me and would say, "Mr. Mathews I've got to go to college." He was just determined. His teachers and counselors had written him letters, saying that he was qualified and eligible to enter any college in America. I knew I needed to help him get to college."

"I drove him around for a month, trying to get resources to help him. Eventually, Committeeman Leroy Tyus wrote a letter to McDonnell Douglas on his behalf, and they hired him in March. By September, he had enough money to go on to college. He excelled so much that a business corporation paid his way to law school. He sent all three of his kids to law school. Coming together to help our children is essential, because all young people need a support system to achieve their goals. He has a very successful law firm today; he is Attorney Taylor Fields, of Kansas City."

What do you recommend to people when they are trying to build community advocacy, and are looking for support or wanting to share their message with others?

1. **Your message has to come from within your heart, mind, and soul**. You have to be an example of what you are trying to teach.

2. **You must be sincere, honest and full of humility.** People will invest in your purpose and your dreams when they believe in you.

3. **Be an example.** Show people who you are, where you stand, that you are willing to work hard, and that people can count on you. I see the late President Ronald Reagan and President Barack Obama as examples of this. With clear intention and a work ethic, you really can achieve your goals.

4. **Seek out partners with a common purpose.** Churches are one the best resources to present and/or receive information, because of their mission to provide educational and social resources for parishioners and the community at-large.

Five Personal Steps to Achieving Extraordinary Results from Martin Luther Mathews:

1. **Be honest with yourself.** Know what your ability is and use your resources to help others.

2. **Make personal eye-to-eye contact.** Appropriate body language is important to make people comfortable and help them buy in to your message.

3. **Always deliver on your promises.** People watch what you say and do. Excuses are not acceptable.

4. **Sacrifice comes with success.** Jesus sacrificed his own life on the cross for our salvation.

   "Even though I've had disappointments and roadblocks—we kept going."

5. **Be direct, firm, to the point and have confidence in yourself.**

"Organizations must be equipped with 21st Century technology to continue to attract young people, especially our churches."

"Technology has definitely impacted our world and the way we connect to each other today. Non-profits and churches must embrace this technology to spread their message."

"By being able to read, use the Internet and watch TV, we can learn about places and people all over the world. We learn that the Jerusalem mentioned in the scripture is a real place that we can visit on this earth."

"Finally, you must believe in yourself; then you will be able to believe in others."

"A quality education and strong people skills are the solid foundation of success."

"In Matthew 5:16, it is written, "Let your light so shine before men, that they may see your **good works** and glorify your Father in heaven.""

Martin Luther Mathews, Co-Founder, President, and CEO of the Mathews-Dickey Boys' & Girls' Club, has always had an agenda for the best for kids.

*The views and opinions expressed in this section are solely those of Martin Luther Mathews and do not represent the views or opinions of the Mathews-Dickey Boys' & Girls' Club.

Establishing Legacies (Relationship/Spirituality)
"Don't look for reason to break up look
for reasons to stay together."
Clyde Ruffin

Teaching and Loving
Pastor and Professor Clyde Ruffin

Professor Clyde Ruffin is pretty close to retirement. He has influenced and inspired countless young people during his now second term as the Chair of the Department of Theatre at the University of Missouri-Columbia. He serves as Senior Pastor of Second Missionary Baptist Church, also in Columbia.

Pastor Ruffin is brilliant, humble, and meticulous. He's a lover of the arts and of the Word of God. He looks forward to continuing to share his life's works because he knows his true calling is to teach.

Professor Ruffin could have spent his life performing on stages around the world because he's that good; yet, he has invested in giving thousands the tools to live their purpose.

Though he probably wouldn't tell you, he's been a preacher almost his entire life. But, it's no surprise. It shows. It's remarkable when a person knows who he/she is—and *whose* and can simply express it without pretense.

Pastor Ruffin Shares:

"I enjoy the feeling that I have been able to inspire others to achieve and to have confidence. I think I have been a good father, and an ok husband (to my wife, Sheila), and I love them all!"

Questions Asked of Pastor Ruffin:
How did you get through 33 years of Marriage?

1. I/We don't look for reason to break up; we look for reasons to stay together.

2. Having the commitment to stay together is not without bumps. Don't expect it to be.

3. The greatest thing is to give each other the space to be whom they are—to learn to accept the other person, faults and all—and to prayerfully accept differences.

4. Quickly identify what is worth fighting about. Figure out what you should let go.

5. Do not enable the other person's weaknesses. It is hard to undo those after so many years.

6. Make a commitment to learn what makes the other person feel loved, and teach the other person to do that with you—rather than simply expecting them to respect, give, or receive

without demonstration from you.

Be aware of the "Five Love Languages." Sometimes you may be "speaking different languages." The languages are:
1. *Words of Affirmation*
2. *Quality Time*
3. *Receiving Gifts*
4. *Acts of Service*
5. *Physical Touch*

Quality time is so important because, if you don't give it, the other person may feel abandoned.

In addition, each should have personal, individual interests—an idle mind is likely to feel abandoned, too.

Gary Chapman wrote the book *The 5 Love Languages*. If you are interested in learning more about this subject or taking a "quiz" to see how you rank, you can go to his site, *www.5lovelanguages.com.*

You can learn more about Pastor Ruffin's life and his calling on at www.2ndbc.com. He will also be featured in the upcoming, "If You Really Want to…" College Student Guide…coming soon!

Chapter 16

Faith and Communication Considerations
Jo Lena Johnson

*"Jesus turned and saw her. "Take heart, daughter,"
he said, "your faith has healed you." And the
woman was healed from that moment,"*
Matthew 9:22 (NIV)

FAITH—Scripture says, *"Now faith is the substance of things hoped for, the evidence of things not seen"* in Hebrews 11:1. If you take a look at the rest of Chapter 11, you'll notice thirty-nine additional verses, which show us who actually took God at His word. It's helpful because some of the people in the Bible felt similar to how you may feel—human (because they were human). The verses chronicle the lives of Abel, Noah, Abraham and Sarah all the way through Joshua and other champions of faith.

Hebrews 11:30 says, *"By faith the walls of Jericho fell down, after they were compassed about seven days."* God gave some specific instructions about how to conquer the city of Jericho, and it's a victorious tale of steadfastness, unity and the almighty power of God—as the people, lead by Joshua, used their voices to destroy the strongholds.

What are strongholds in your life that need to be loosed? Think about relationships, habits, or past "stuff" which may be in your way and delaying your victory. Take a look at Joshua 6:1–27 to see one instance of how God's hand will utterly destroy those concerns, which are not yours to bear.

> *"Jesus said to the woman, "Your faith*
> *has saved you; go in peace."*
> Luke 7:50 (NIV)

<u>The Revealing Word</u> also says, *"Faith is more than mere belief. It is the very substance of that which is believed. It works by love. Thoughts of condemnation, enmity, and resistance must be released, and divine love declared; then faith will work unhindered."*

In other words, "to have faith in God is to have the faith of God. We must have faith in God as our Father and source of all the good we desire." Note the following story:

The Withered Fig Tree
"Early the next morning Jesus was returning to the city.
He was hungry. Seeing a lone fig tree alongside the road,
he approached it anticipating a breakfast of figs.
When he got to the tree, there was nothing but fig leaves.
He said, "No more figs from this tree—ever!"
The fig tree withered on the spot, a dry
stick. The disciples saw it happen.
They rubbed their eyes, saying,
"Did we really see this?
A leafy tree one minute, a dry stick the next?"

But Jesus was matter-of-fact:
"Yes—and if you embrace this kingdom
life and don't doubt God,
you'll not only do minor feats like I did to the fig tree,
but also triumph over huge obstacles.

This mountain, for instance, you'll tell,
'Go jump in the lake,' and it will jump.
Absolutely everything, ranging from small to large,
as you, make it a part of your believing prayer,
gets included as you lay hold of God."
Matthew 21:20–22 (The Message Bible)

Business Blessings
Gail Day

Gail Day Shares:

"I've been a Salon Owner for eight years. As the economy changed, especially in 2009, so did the frequency of the business. Fewer clients were coming, and coming less regularly. The building owner wanted to increase the amount of my lease for the upcoming year. I had a choice, and I chose to close the shop on January 31, 2010."

"I gave my operators a two-month notice so that they could reestablish themselves somewhere else. One said, 'I'll stay with you until the end,' and the others left. Thirty days before I was due to close, the building owner said, 'Name your price,' and I immediately knew that happened by the Grace of God."

I looked at the ceiling and said, 'Thank you, God.' ...I did it, I named my price. I have a 'new salon' in the 'same location' filled with talented, cooperative people who each love the Lord, just like me!"

Mrs. Day continues:
Five Ways God has Blessed my Business

1. He lowered my rent. It's more affordable and less of a struggle.

2. He's increased my clientele.

3. He sent me team players to work with in this environment.

4. Every time I've been in a crunch, He's carried me. And, I know it's Him.

5. He blessed me so that everyone saw my blessings, and in that I believe, someone else got a blessing. Someone's faith had to grow by demonstration through my circumstances.

Ms. Day says,

"This experience has taught me to get out of His way, the quicker I do that, the better off I am. Every day, 3–4 times a day, I walk around this salon and say, "Thank You Jesus." It's remarkable, astonishing when God shows favor."

"And, I'm adding this—if you sit still and wait on Him, it'll be right on time!"

Beauty and a Day Salon is located at 515 N Taylor Ave in the Central West End of St. Louis, Missouri.

When you stop by or call Gail, please send our best to her!

And if, according to Jesus, our faith could be as powerful as that, imagine the Lord's Faith…God's faithfulness endures forever!

∞

From the Message Bible: Psalm 117

God's Faithfulness Endures Forever
Praise God, everybody! Applaud God, all people!
His love has taken over our lives;
God's faithful ways are eternal.
Hallelujah!

More Definitions for Your Consideration and Application
What are they Talking About?

The following are some simple terms that you hear in many formal church settings. When you read the definition, ask yourself the question, "How can I best use or accomplish this in my daily life?" and begin to make choices for you. Being clear about your destination causes exponential growth and *extraordinary* results!

If people were willing, they would often ask these questions:

1. What do they mean?

2. Why is this important to me? (benefits)

3. How do we do it?

4. What difference can *doing* make?

Defining and Applying "Church Words"—(Source: The Revealing Word)

1. **Praise**—The quality of mind that eulogizes the good; one of the avenues through which spirituality expresses.

2. **Prayer**—Communion between God and man. This communion takes place in the innermost part of man's being. It is the only way to cleanse and perfect the consciousness and, thus, permanently heal the body.

3. **Worship**—When one worships, he bestows His love *on*, or identifies himself *with*, the things of Spirit. Worship represents the efforts of man to sustain a right mental attitude toward God.

4. **Meditation**—Continuous and contemplative thought to dwell mentally on anything; realizing the reality of the Absolute; a steady effort of the mind to know God; man's spiritual approach to God.

> *"But the fruit of the Spirit is love, joy, peace, patience, kindness, goodness, faithfulness, gentleness, and self-control. Against such things, there is no law."*
> Galatians 5:22–24 (NIV)

How clean are your filters?

When it comes to things of Spirit, sometimes our "filters" can get in the way. The good news is, if you realize that you suffer interference from your filters, you can "hear" and "see" past them.

The Four Human Filters are:
1. Looking Good
2. Avoiding Pain
3. Being in Control
4. Being Right

*Now...*Let's talk door screens—they keep things out, and they let some things in. Sometimes the screens are brand new, freshly hung, clean and easy to open and close. Sometimes they have been hanging for over 40 years and have never been patched, cleaned, or repaired.

What might be the difference between the first and second screen? Do they serve the same purpose? Do they work equally as well? Why or why not? What's the purpose of a front door screen? What does it do? Well, just like those screen doors, we all, as humans, have "screens" or filters. We actually have four of them. And, just like those screen doors, they let some things in and keep some things out. They serve as protection, comfort and make up our self-esteem/self-concept and directly affect our thoughts, attitudes—and especially our actions.

Once we understand that sometimes our screens are blocking growth, success; or us from our good or from harmony, connection or productivity, we can open the door to new possibilities, discovery, change, adventure, and rewards of all kinds. The challenge is that often times we are blind to how our filters are impacting our views, values, and choices, and ultimately our lives. And, everyone's perspective is unique.

So, when thinking about our "filters" or screens, keep in mind that each person's experience is individual and will somehow "look different."

> *"Removing the "Old Stuff" takes Willingness,*
> *Choice and Objectivity or Openness."*
> *Jo Lena Johnson*

For example, if you did not grow up *chatting with*—not <u>*texting to*</u>—people, playing sports, reading books, cutting grass, babysitting for extra cash, riding your bicycle around the neighborhood, playing 45's, 78's, 8 tracks or cassettes; or not attending—and certainly not being allowed to attend—Rated R movies until you were over 17; but using correction tape with a typewriter, using the telephone book, calling people to get directions before long road trips or short ones to their house ...

Your filters are likely going to be quite different from those who did—again, experiences. You've heard the stories, right?

"When I was your age I had to walk 35 miles to and from school every single day..." or "Back in my time, women, were housewives, secretaries or babysitters..." or "Pull yourself up by your bootstraps!"

Yes, they said it.

Well, if you can relate in any way to one of those statements, you were likely not born in the 1990's or 2000's! If you, me or anyone else is going to get beyond the limitations of our filters, it will oftentimes take a painstaking process and the "hope," "dream," or "wish" of high reward. And, because there are likely people in your life who "care" about you, they probably don't mention certain things, or even address them because "they know how you are" or "they already know how you will respond."

One of the biggest downfalls of our filters is sheer insanity: Doing the same things over and over again, and expecting somehow to get different results. Our filters keep us misguided, super comfy and oftentimes stuck! Nobody wants to be the bearer of bad news...and nobody just NEEDS some extra work, or do we?

As you begin to acknowledge that the filters exist, become aware of the opportunities for growth and the benefits (likely short term) of keeping them securely in place. And lastly, keep practicing. You might find ways to expand, explore, discover and thrive...Only if you are willing!

Willingness—Choice—Take a Stand

"Happy is like a tent — Joy is like a home.
If I know joy, I can get through the times that make me unhappy.
Emotions are like tents — they are temporary.
Feelings are home. Joy is everlasting."
Jo Lena Johnson

I also say...

- Be a good spirited communicator and leader.

- When you are true to yourself, you will shine.

- You must believe in something or someone higher than your little self:

    o The Ideal, the Creator, the Master, the Life Giver, the Lighter, and the Keeper of the flame.

- To be successful I must be consistent!

    o "Successful" can mean money, title, roles, goals, family, life, time, and service.

    o Consistent, yet flexible...Flexible in every situation so that my actions and attitudes will always follow right, not my temperament of the moment.

- Because it's different, it won't be perfect.

- You must be willing to move <u>through</u> and <u>past</u>.

- You must be trustworthy. It does not mean doing it all or being perfect, but it does mean being honest with yourself and others, when your schedule or "plate" is overloaded and you need help to grow, complete, and still keep your sanity.

"Forgiveness is Not an Option; It Is Required"
Reverend Dr. William H. Knight

"There are a lot of things that we <u>think</u> we want...Is there space for those things that you <u>say</u> you want? When our lives are so full with the things we 'have to' do, very often there is no room for what we feel we...ought to' do."
Dr. William Knight

The Reverend William H. Knight grew up Cleveland, Ohio, where he says, "The winters are intense and the summers are even more so." He was determined to be in "show business" and was passionately interested in pursuing theatre. He moved to Northern California in 1961, enrolled in college, and ended up joining the Navy in 1962. He visited places he would not have seen otherwise, as it was during the very beginning of the Viet Nam Conflict. Timing was key to his expanded worldview. His adventures led him to Singapore, Thailand, Hong King, and the Philippines where he learned about people, about new ways of doing things, and about living all along the way.

He admits that he had known that "sharing God's Love and God's Truth" had been part of his destiny for a very long time; however, it took him a while to make it "official." He credits his time in Hollywood as part of creating who he is today and knows that each experience has contributed to his feelings of being extraordinarily blessed.

By 1987, Reverend William had been working in Los Angeles for years while living his show biz dream. He had enrolled in a workshop to enhance his acting pursuits when a couple from England told him of classes taught by "an extraordinary woman who was an entertainer." They were speaking about Reverend Della Reese, (of *Touched by An Angel*). When, after much resistance and "false starts" to being on his purpose-driven path he finally went to Rev. Della's class, she was teaching an approach to spirituality and relationship with God, which so appealed to him that, instantaneously, he knew that being involved was something he needed to do. That meeting led him to work with Rev. Della for 23 years.

Reverend Della's vision of her destiny to serve God led to her founding the Understanding Principles for Better Living Church (UP). The Reverend Delores Francine McMillan, was a highly regarded and extraordinary Bible scholar who was also in pursuit of a "new life." She had served under the Rev. Johnnie Colemon at Christ Universal Temple in Chicago, which led to her becoming Rev. Della's Assistant Minister at UP Church. Rev. Mac was an obedient woman, bound and determined that Rev. William was to accept his purpose, which meant he had to be ordained; and so he was, in 1995.

We share these details because we want you to know that the people, the experiences, and the least likely turns and interactions, in the midst of our daily life, can turn a dull day into the one moment that has been awaiting you—the awakening, purposeful, and clear path to your *Extraordinary* Living—if you *really* want to!

Reverend William Knight Shares:

When I finished my tour in the Navy, I settled in Northern California, and graduated with a degree in Speech and Drama from Cal State University at Hayward. I did this at the behest of my sister who insisted that I have some formal training to "fall back on," in case I didn't turn out to be the next Sidney Poitier.

I was fortunate in that I made my professional debut in a stage production of *The Fantastiks.* It was around 1967–68, and there was a lot of unrest on most college campuses. To calm some of the tensions at Cal State, the University wanted to offer courses specifically designed to engage African-American students. Having only a BA degree, I was offered a full time faculty position in the Speech/Drama Department for the 1968–1969 academic year. After one full school year, I decided that teaching didn't give me the kind of fulfillment I desired; so, I moved to Los Angeles to play in the "big pond."

He continues:
Three Considerations when Pursuing Your Purpose

1. **Your Divine Purpose.** Accepting and recognizing that you have a Divine Purpose is your God given destiny. Until you are willing to confront, acknowledge, and accept it, you will never be truly fulfilled. You can deny or even reject it, but it will never go away. It cannot go away because it is the truth of who you are. It's not something you do; it's a part of who you are. Until you fully accept that, you can never be true to yourself.

    As much as I tried to resist the call to teach, every time I turned around there it was, another opportunity to teach. I had to accept that one of my callings was to be a teacher.

2. **Encouragement from People.** I learned that not everyone who offers you encouragement is capable of moving you toward your goal. They can only encourage you for what they see according to what they think you should be.

My colleagues were eagerly encouraging me to be a college teacher. They saw my being productive and doing well; however, it didn't fulfill my soul. While they were loving and honest, they could not give me the real desire of my heart. At that time, I didn't know what it was; however, I knew it wasn't being a college teacher.

3. **Limitations are often Self-Imposed.** As painful as it may be, most of the time, it is necessary to leave your comfort zone in order to pursue your highest goal. Many people experience limitations not due to other people, but due to those that are self-imposed.

I had developed a network of friends, a professional network, a comfortable living situation, and everything I thought necessary. The only thing that wasn't available was how to reach my higher goal, to live my destined calling. It wasn't on the campus or in Northern California.

Four New Thoughts about Pursuing Your Dreams

1. **Divine Discontent Happens:** You must be willing to interrupt your life as it is, by acting on the urging of your soul. No matter how well things seem to be going, you cannot be satisfied because there is a higher purpose not being fulfilled.

2. **Releasing Your True Self:** You must be willing to accept that releasing what you have is not restricting you. Not

opening up to the possibility of having something greater is resulting in less.

3. **Greater Vision of Ourselves:** As human creature, we tend to be territorial, which is how we typically limit and define ourselves. Know that, if are we are going to have a greater experience of life; we must have a greater vision of ourselves.

    You must be able to survive and prevail in the "big pond."

4. **Giving up Fear:** You must give up fear. You cannot have determination and retain fear at the same time. As you examine the full situations and concerns, realize that the biggest is probably overcoming fear.

    I had to overcome the fear that I could not be enough or do enough to survive. I had to stop thinking I wouldn't make it. The negative thoughts had to be overcome by my absolute believing that God would not urge me into a path that was not going to be successful.

My reality was I had been placed in situations that constantly made me aware that there was a spiritual component in life (my calling), *and I did not want to* answer. The calling seemed an adjunct to what I was doing at the moment. But, it kept showing up, knocking; and eventually I had to answer the call.

Hollywood Highlights—Pursuing my Dream Without Waiting Tables

I was able to be supported professionally in so many aspects of "show biz" in California. In the past, I have been a producer, director, and writer of musicals. I have done TV; radio; voice-overs, including cartoon voice-overs. There is little in the realm of motion pictures, theatre, and television that I haven't done. These have been big blessings throughout my career. Such endeavors allowed me to have a career free of waiting tables to sustain myself. There is nothing wrong with waiting tables; it just wasn't part of my path. My Hollywood experience was part of creating who I am at this moment. Without each past experience, *I wouldn't have or be what I have and am now.* All is contingent upon all that had happened in the past through the people I've met, the experiences I've had, and the perspective from which I see my life and "living." I view it all as an extraordinary blessing because I feel extraordinarily blessed.

Eight Ways I Learned to Approach God

1. God is not an old crotchety bearded man in the clouds, waiting to throw thunderbolts when you make a mistake.

2. You are not—I am not—a miserable sinner, born in sin with only a life of sin for which to look forward.

3. Your life was not created so that you could suffer more than someone else in a "suffering" contest.

4. God does not have love, God *is* Love! And so, whatever experience of love we have ever had, has been an experience of God.

5. God lives, moves, and has being in each one of us. We are expressions of God made manifest. The reality of who I am, and who you are, is not limited to solely what I and others see.

   The essence of each of us is God pressed out, or "expressed." And, that this is true of us, no matter what path we choose.

Our spiritual expression—regardless of our religious training—presents the reality that we are all God's children. He shows up in all that I say and all that I do…and for you, too. We can never escape because we are in the image and likeness of God, that's who we are. This is big! It took a great deal of prayer and meditation for me to come to this understanding.

6. Love is not something you say; love is something you do. For example, Jesus said, *"How can you say you love God whom you have never seen, and say that you hate your brother that you see daily?"* (1 Peter 1:8). Hatred, intolerance, and judgment are ungodly. Knowingly, you cannot participate in those behaviors while claiming to cling to God's love. They are incompatible with Truth…This is one of the most important concepts of living a good life.

7. *Forgiveness is not an option—it is required.* Because the definitive prayer of Jesus tells us how we are to communicate and commune with God. The prayer "forgive us our trespasses" clearly states in order to obtain forgiveness, I must be willing to extend forgiveness.

8. Most of us spend our lives focusing on our own needs, but the Law (the Lord) says, *"As you give, so shall you receive."* That is the Law of Sowing and Reaping. If I am not willing to sow in my life, how can I then expect my life to reap a great harvest? In order for us to live fulfilling lives, we have to look for ways we can give, and then be willing to give in the ways we can. Do not overlook the obvious; there is always something that you can give. *The very thing that you perceive to be your greatest need is the thing you must be willing to give in a greater way.*

Truth, for me, is that which is eternal, everlasting, and unchanging. Truth is also a synonym for "unchanging." Understand that even facts change, but the Truth cannot and does not change. For me God is <u>the entire</u> Universe, which means there is nothing that can't be. God's not going to withhold anything that I *really* need to know. And, I don't *really* need to know why jet airplanes don't fall, I just need to know how to buy the ticket.

Something else to consider…you don't get what you (simply) want; you always get what you truly expect. Because you might want a whole lot of stuff but those are transient thoughts. That "stuff" doesn't or shouldn't have the force of your convictions behind them. The more emotional energy you invest in your expectation (what you *really* want), the more you empower its showing up in your life.

It's important that we don't assume that people know what we know.

This is another of the most profound lessons I've learned in my spiritual journey. What tangible ways are you preparing for your goal, other than wishing and hoping? If you *really* believe that something is part of your purpose, your destiny, and part of your journey, you have to make preparation for it. Your responsibility is to prepare, and then you must allow God to move. Be willing to push yourself into action.

Reverend William answers…What I *Really* want people to know about God…

The instant that you are willing to seek God, He is available. It is not a matter of climbing the highest mountain. He is available in that instant you are willing to seek Him because He abides within each one of us. As Paul said, He is *"closer than breathing"* in Galatians 2:15–21. And, as Jesus said, *"the Father and I are one"* (John 10:25–30).

Visit www.BeExtraordinaryBook.com to learn more from Dr. William Knight.

Chapter 17

Conflict, Sam, and Living Extraordinarily
Jo Lena Johnson

Creating Legacies through Connecting
Wisdom, Experience, and Good People

I believe that if you know what you *really* want and are crystal clear on what you don't know, do know, and would like to know; and if you are totally prepared, you should be able to "capture" a wise message in a sixty-minute phone conversation. This would happen, especially if all parties were willing, trusting, and open to communicate. As Dr. Jefferson indicated, "mentorship" is crucial to success—as well as listening and applying what you learn in order to "be yourself."

I started the series *"If You Really Want to..."* because I *really* want people to have access. I asked God to show me how I could serve Him, and serve people, while being who He intends me to be. Too many times, I have been saddened because I see greatness in people, and yet each of us continues to struggle for one reason or another.

I know so many talented people who are up to great things. They are already living certain aspects of their lives in extraordinary ways. And, with a well-placed phone call, a letter of recommendation, or even a heart-felt email, we are living up to Jesus' command: "to love one another." He's working with them and me in my life, answering prayer in undeniably, wonderful, and marvelous ways. My prayer for you is that you get what you need through the reading this book, and others like it.

I also want you to know that I try to live up to what I share, and that I struggle too. Though I share a bit about my early years in the back of the book, I *really* want you to meet and benefit from two other great people that I'm honored to know.

You already heard from them earlier. Instead, of writing another introduction about them, I have chosen to share an email, as an introduction, that I actually sent to both of them originally.

I had committed to being on the call with them. At the time, I was challenged with some things in my personal life, and I just needed some time for myself. However, they needed to meet.

I asked God that night to help me to "fulfill my commitment" to "connect" with them, and to help me not have to be on the phone. A few minutes later, I sat at my computer and sent them this email. I thank God for the words and for their "connection."

> *From:* Jo Lena Johnson
> *Sent:* Saturday, August 29, 2009 1:21 AM
> *To:* Kevin Fleming; Daryl Whittington
> *Subject:* Preparation & The Message
>
> *Kevin—you are an excellent teacher—in that you have a lot of experience and capability to explain not only the content, but also the context—why it matters.*
>
> *I appreciate you because you taught me: to be confident, to not take things so personally, to calm down, that I needed to beware of the way I was talking to people—especially men.*
>
> *Finally, I'm becoming able to express myself and believe*

that I can somehow make a difference in this world, not just because I work hard and use my mouth; but because your compassion, empathy and moral character showed me that there might actually be a man on the planet who would love me—you didn't "quit me," in this case "fire me" when I messed up… I didn't realize how the way I was speaking to Jerome (big tough and strong), was causing him to feel uncomfortable and, thus, battle me….

Daryl, I was very frustrated when I worked for Kevin—I didn't "fit in" with the other people who were around and I struggled—yes I did a good job but, I didn't know how to treat people…so, one day, I decided to quit the station go to another job. It was a great job in title and responsibility, I was Promotion Manager for the Los Angeles Philharmonic and the Hollywood Bowl! And, I hated it (the people were great and the place was great—it just wasn't for me at the time). I was so afraid because I didn't know what to do— and I felt I had made a mistake. One day, I called Kevin and "inquired" as to what was happening at the station—I was afraid and I needed GUIDANCE and EMPATHY and Kevin allowed me to have my old job back.

Most "bosses" would never do that. If nothing else but for pride/ego. Back then, I didn't appreciate how Kevin even "creatively" got sponsorship to pay for my salary. He could have easily turned his back on me but, he didn't.

All of us make mistakes—and unfortunately, we don't often have access to the experienced wisdom and knowledge of someone who could possibly prepare us for our undertaking.

Kevin doesn't even realize how much he has to share—the depth and the fiber and the way his presence has affected, prepared and fortified SO MANY.

Kevin, Daryl is not only a smart, bright, eager and humble person—he is also a young minister—now that he is entering the radio business, I would like him to be as prepared for the environment and how it works so that he can "create substance" that St. Louis and East St. Louis truly need and deserve. For however long, Daryl gets to just be himself—and that will be enough—armed with a few kernels of wisdom. Then he can—and probably will—make some mistakes—but at least not the same ones "we made" and perhaps without the high costs.

Somehow, I know that by connecting you two, it will be good for you—not just the content about the radio stuff but also because you both are similar. You have gone through life changing experiences that could have defeated you—yet, you remain open, loving kind and willing.

Because of each of you, there have and will continue to be young people, older people and others who will feel better about themselves just because they know you—I know I sure do! Soon, by the Grace of God more people will start to experience joy again, appreciation again and skills.

Please, have a great phone call with each other, hope you will connect without me on the phone, I'm spent—and now, you have already been introduced. I just need to rejuvenate—and you guys can handle it!

Though I was "in radio" for a little while as Promotion Director of KACE in Los Angeles, my experience didn't "qualify" me to provide Daryl the insight, depth or breadth that he deserved. However, I knew who could help, and I knew that I had to be willing to ask…if it were going to happen.

Then, there's Sam…Who is Sam?

"Sam" could be "Samantha or Samuel"—or Betty. Sam is a name I made up to help people with perspective. Think of someone you find difficult—either they seem difficult or you might find it difficult when dealing with a challenging situation with them. Your "Sam" may be someone who you inherited/they might be related to you— like a parent or child; or, perhaps "Sam" could be someone that you're in a relationship with, like a partner or spouse—you love them; they love you, *but they are still difficult.* "Sam" could also be someone with whom you work.

You may not want to deal with Sam; however, they may not be going anywhere. Sam may affect your current or your future results; so, it's your choice of how to handle things with Sam. I recommend choosing open body language, appropriate tone of voice, and watching the words you choose.

The main thing is, get off "autopilot:" When you see Sam coming, you might think, "Oh no, here we go again." However, if you're thinking, "Oh no, here we go again," guess what will probably happen again? It's called conditioned response. It often happens because, in the past, we had a negative experience. Something in our heads tells us, "It's going to happen again." While I say it's your choice that it doesn't have to happen again, are you *really* willing to do something different?

A "Mantra" for Dealing with Sam

"Some conflict will never be resolved."

Do you believe it? Do you like it? Please try this…

"Some conflict will never be resolved to my satisfaction."

Do you believe it? Do you like it? Is this the same as the first statement? (No!)…Here's the big one, and I'm glad you can't see me to throw something at me:

"Some conflict will never be resolved to my satisfaction—especially with Sam!"

Try repeating that 3 times. Let it settle...

> *"Some conflict will never be resolved to my satisfaction—especially with Sam!" "Some conflict will never be resolved to my satisfaction—especially with Sam!" "Some conflict will never be resolved to my satisfaction—especially with Sam!"*

Are you willing to choose?

Most of the time, it's not about satisfaction. I don't like it because I *want to* be satisfied! However, it is about choice.

If you are willing to focus on what's *really* important, or what *really* matters, you may be able to objectively separate fact from interpretation (Be Patient and Kind).

You may make choices about keeping Sam around, letting Sam go, or creating a mental (and perhaps physical) space where both you and Sam can co-exist through the conflict.

Affirmation for a "Clean Slate": Warning—it Works!

Besides the Sam Mantra, I have an affirmation/prayer for you—if you *really* want to have someone exit from your life. I got this from Reverend Mac; she was kind enough to share it at a time when I *really* needed it. I occasionally have to pull it out, and throughout the years, I have shared it with some "friends in need," as well.

But, I must warn you—and this is because it's so powerful. You might be focused on a "particular Sam;" however, if you have other Sam's that you have been keeping around, they could fall off too. Maybe you aren't "quite" ready for that to happen.

Here it is:

> *I (lovingly) claim the (peaceful) exit from my life*
> *of all those who are not for my highest good—they*
> *fade from my life and prosper somewhere else.*
> Courtesy of the late Rev. Delores F. Mc Millan

> *(I'm not sure, if she originated this statement,*
> *or if she simply passed it on to me.)*

Memorize it. Work with it, and let it work with you. If you are in a situation where your thoughts keep going back to a person, a place, or a thing that is no longer "good for you;" it may be the very "thing" that is impeding you on your extraordinary journey.

How to Get Through Some of Life's Toughest Challenges...

- Pray.

- Read the Bible.

- Ask a trusted, experienced, and proven source for guidance, wisdom, and patience in reaching your goals.

- Be willing to listen to what is being said and what is not said. Be willing to watch for what is done and what is not done. That is, the facts, not the interpretation.

- Be principle-centered and purpose-driven through your misery, through your hurt, through your confusion, through politics, and always *to* your hard work!

- Avoid politics, including games, leveraging, power struggles, insecurities, selfishness, and low self-esteem.

- Serve. Service is important; it is necessary; just like you!

- Believe in miracles. They do happen. This book in your hand is a miracle for me!

Daily Reminders, Especially When the "Going Gets Tough"

- Focus on those whom you feel can best be benefited by you.

- Show empathy and compassion for others, even when they "act up."

- Show passion, courage, respect, awareness, appreciation, and responsibility to rule obstacles.

- Give freely while setting and maintaining your personal and professional boundaries.

- Be resourceful. Don't assume you'll always have the money, time, or support from human beings. You won't!

- Work to establish equity (fairness).

Cotton Pickin' Leadership—
Five Life Lessons
Maida Coleman

Pickin' Cotton All the Way to State Government

Maida Coleman shares what she learned picking cotton:

Sure, I'm a country girl...I chopped cotton, picked cotton, chopped beans and got up at 4 a.m. to go to work. There was something redeeming about having my own money. It wasn't easy—just like life...and, what I really want you to know is that we are in it together.

I'll share five lessons for life, which you can use to make your life fuller, complete, or tolerable. It'll take some work from you. After all, we're talking about "Cotton Pickin' Leadership!

Maida Coleman's Five Cotton Pickin' Life Lessons

1. I learned about life, survival and the importance of independence and interdependence.

2. I learned my strengths, and the ability to persevere.

3. I learned to appreciate my elders, and what they could teach me.

4. I learned the joy of having my own money that *I* earned. It was like being self-employed.

5. I learned, as in the fields, we are all in this together—groups of people. Things we had in common were straw hats, tools for cutting, and sweat rags; and we were huddled together, heading to the fields—just trying to make it.

Lincoln University started in late August, right about the time we finished chopping cotton before the fall harvest. My cousin Annette told me that she was getting $60 a week to chop cotton. Wow! $60 a week was big money to an 18-year-old girl. Hence, while working two part-time jobs, and being a full-time student, I remember thinking about dropping out of college to go home and pick cotton. However, my experiences helped me to remain steadfast and to keep going. I ran for State Senate because I wanted to make a difference. I was able to accomplish so much good while I was in office. After I reached my term limit, I desired to continue my career in public service so, I ran for Mayor of the City of St. Louis because I care about people's well-being…and I understand that we are all in this together—groups of people.

Why I Ran for Mayor

1. Honesty and integrity are important to me and I wanted to bring those elements with me into city government.

2. I felt someone needed to stand up for the people without a voice who were not being represented.

3. I wanted to help bring the city to a place where diversity is embraced—racially and economically, in order to build relationships and reduce misunderstandings…

4. I wanted to create programs, which provide a safe and comfortable living environment in St. Louis City.

Though I did not win my bid to become mayor, by running in the race, some real issues were addressed that may not have happened otherwise.

I thought about my goals in life, my hopes, and dreams. Then, I asked God to guide and direct me. In the past, I had been overwhelmed with distractions and decided that I wanted to figure out what I could do to have a better, less hectic and prosperous life. I asked the Universe "What do I really want to do? What can I do to meet my needs financially and bring self satisfaction?"

The definitive answer came to me as clear as day: I want to be a speaker, motivator. I want to write books that bring joy to people, travel the world promoting my books, and have them become movies. I thought, "Can I really do this?" The answer was, "It is done. Now do your part."

At this point in my life, I am following His directions to move to the next level and I am finally motivated, I know that with a time frame, God's guidance, and my faith, that "Cotton Pickin' " tenacity is helping me through.

*Maida Coleman has spent some time as a freelance writer and she is an author-in-process. In addition to her passion for writing, she has exercised fervor for citizens' rights and the **law by having served in the Missouri House of Representatives as a State Senator for eight years (2001–2009).** She remains a successful, well-respected woman who served her constituency with integrity, commitment, and dedication. After this initial interview, she took on a new role—she is now the Missouri Department of Labor and Industrial Relations, Division of Employment Security, Designated Principal/Liaison. Yes, that's a long title—and fitting for this extraordinary woman! In this role, she continues to provide public service to the State of Missouri and to live in her vision, take action, and produce great results! Congratulations, Ms. Coleman!*

Chapter 18

Resources for You to Take Action!
Dr. L. Jefferson and J. Johnson

If you really want to know more, pick up the Bible and read!

Why <u>Read</u> the Holy Bible?

There are many practical benefits, which have been covered throughout this book, and if we didn't say it clearly before, God shares His will for our lives through His Word. You will *find some basic, practical tips to grow* through your own adventurous journey of the Bible.

Let's Explore!

Did you know? The Bible is made up of 66 books. They are arranged as follows:

The Old Testament: Books 1 to 39
The New Testament: Books 40 to 66.

Books of Law ~ Written by Moses
1. Genesis
2. Exodus
3. Leviticus
4. Numbers
5. Deuteronomy

Books of History ~ Old Testament Narrative

6. Joshua
7. Judges
8. Ruth
9. 1 Samuel
10. 2 Samuel
11. 1 Kings
12. 2 Kings
13. 1 Chronicles
14. 2 Chronicles
15. Ezra
16. Nehemiah
17. Esther

Books of Poetry ~ Wisdom Literature

18. Job
19. Psalms
20. Proverbs
21. Ecclesiastes
22. Songs of Solomon

The Major Prophets

23. Isaiah
24. Jeremiah
25. Lamentations
26. Ezekiel
27. Daniel

The Minor Prophets

28. Hosea
29. Joel
30. Amos
31. Obadiah

32. Jonah
33. Micah
34. Nahum
35. Habakkuk
36. Zephaniah
37. Haggai
38. Zechariah
39. Malachi

The Gospels (Good News) ~ New Testament Narratives
40. Matthew
41. Mark
42. Luke
43. John

History ~ New Testament Narrative
44. Acts

Letters (Epistles) from Paul
45. Romans
46. 1 Corinthians
47. 2 Corinthians
48. Galatians
49. Ephesians
50. Philippians
51. Colossians
52. 1 Thessalonians
53. 2 Thessalonians
54. 1 Timothy
55. 2 Timothy
56. Titus
57. Philemon

General Epistles (Letters)

58. Hebrews
59. James
60. 1 Peter
61. 2 Peter
62. 1 John
63. 2 John
64. 3 John
65. Jude

Prophecy Epistle (Apocalyptic Letter) from John

66. Revelation

...YOUR MISSION IS POSSIBLE!...
Jo Lena Johnson

Knowing the Will of God Through the Scriptures

*"And the king stood by a pillar, and made a covenant before the
Lord, to walk after the Lord, and to keep his commandments
and his testimonies and his statutes with all their heart and
all their soul, to perform the words of this covenant that were
written in this book. And all the people stood to the covenant."*
2 Kings 23:3

Covenant = Agreement

Having an agreement with someone is the same as signing a contract.
As we know, it's important to read and review the "terms" of the
contract before signing it. In our culture, it's also recommended that

one "get an attorney" or consult someone who has "authority" in the particular area prior to committing to the agreement.

The things, which we have shared in these pages, have come from our own study, experiences, applied knowledge, interpretations, and use of biblical references. We hope that you have found them timely, relevant, and helpful to you in your life and your journey.

We also know that the best book is the "Good Book," the Holy Bible. We, along with many others, believe that the Holy Bible is the eternal word of God. That being said, this chapter is intended to render the reader a few scriptural references, definitions, and resources as an introduction to or support for the personal journey in exploration to find *God's Will for your life*.

Are you willing to <u>agree</u>?

Do you have a contract with God? One that you understand, can accept, and are capable of fulfilling? Have you ever sat down to read the Bible? It's big and can sometimes be a little intimidating. With time, patience, and understanding, it can also be a spirit-filled journey to self through the power of the Holy Spirit connecting you to God.

This chapter is intended as a gift for you to explore your personal road map (your story and song), through knowing and applying the Will of God to your life through the Scriptures.

What Is the Bible?

The Bible is a library of books, and the purpose of the *written* Word of God (the Bible) is to reveal the *living* Word of God, the Lord Jesus Christ.

2 Timothy 3:14–17 says:

> *"But continue thou in the things which thou hast learned and*
> *hast been assured of, knowing of whom thou hast learned them;*
> *And that from a child (babe) thou hast known the*
> *holy scriptures, which are able to make thee wise unto*
> *salvation through faith which is in Christ Jesus.*
> *All (every holy scripture) is given by inspiration of God,*
> *and is profitable for doctrine, for reproof, for correction,*
> *for instruction in righteousness (right-use-ness):*
> *That the man of God may be perfect, thoroughly*
> *furnished unto all good works."*

The Bible contains certain key numbers, names, places, history, prophecy, philosophy, instruction, inspiration, and wisdom that will help
you live a better life—if you study it, receive it, and follow its guidance.

How Should I <u>Study</u> the Bible?

Start with a prayer…

God, open my mind and heart to Your good and very good. Allow the
Holy Spirit to be my great interpreter that I may <u>know Your Will for me</u>
and my life, in the name of Jesus Christ. Thank you. Amen.

Five Ways to Knowing God's Will for
Your Life—Directly from Scripture

1st – There is a definite will God has for your life:
    "The steps of a good man are ordered by the Lord."
            Psalm 37:23

and

*"I will instruct thee and teach thee in
the way which thou shalt go."*
Psalm 32:8

2nd ~ God desires us to know this will for our lives:
*"Wherefore be ye not unwise, but understanding
what the will of the Lord is."*
Ephesians 5:17

3rd ~ This will is continuous. It does not begin or end at a certain age—God has a will for children, young people, adults, and senior citizens:
*"And the Lord shall guide thee continually, and
satisfy thy soul in drought, and make fat (strong) thy
bones: and thou shalt be like a watered garden, and
like a spring of water, whose waters fail not."*
Isaiah 58:11

4th ~ God's will is specific:
*"And thine ears shall hear a word behind thee,
saying, This is the way, walk ye in it."*
Isaish 30:21

5th ~ God's will is profitable:
"The way of the righteous is made plain."
Proverbs 15:19

and

"This book of the law you shall not forget; but keep it in your
mind day and night, that you may observe to do according
to all that is written therein: for then thou shalt make thy
way prosperous, and then thou shalt have good success."
Joshua 1:8

I study Bible daily, and I have used it as the basis for scriptural research throughout this book. I want to thank the Thomas Nelson Publishers for their thorough documentation in the King James Version of The New Open Bible Study Edition. It is through reading their footnotes that I developed the list above, for our use, though slightly modified so as not to exactly "copy" what they said. I say so because I want to emphasize how important it is to give credit where credit is due.

I am grateful for the journey in my Bible, and I sincerely hope that you, too, find understanding and the answers that you need in yours.

Scripture Related to Christian Living in Five Main Areas of Life
as Chosen by Dr. Lee Roy Jefferson
(Each entry below is from the New International Version, Biblegateway.com)

1. Consider Family:

"Honor your father and your mother, so that you may live
long in the land the LORD your God is giving you."
Exodus 20:12

*"I will instruct you and teach you in the way you
should go; I will counsel you and watch over you."*
Psalm 32:8

*"Wisdom will save you from the ways of wicked men,
from men whose words are perverse, who leave the
straight paths to walk in dark ways, who delight in doing
wrong and rejoice in the perverseness of evil, whose paths
are crooked and who are devious in their ways."*
Proverbs 2:12–15

*"Tell it to your children, and let your children tell it to their
children, and their children to the next generation."*
Joel 1:3

2. Consider Work:

*"Commit to the LORD whatever you do,
and your plans will succeed."*
Proverbs 16:3

*"You and these people who come to you will only wear yourselves
out. The work is too heavy for you; you cannot handle it alone."*
Exodus 18:18

*"I tell you the truth, whatever you bind on earth
will be bound in heaven, and whatever you
loose on earth will be loosed in heaven."*
Matthew 18:18

"For where your treasure is, there your heart will be also."
Matthew 6:21

3. *Consider Finance:*

*"No one can serve two masters. Either he will hate the one
and love the other, or he will be devoted to the one and
despise the other. You cannot serve both God and Money."*
Matthew 6:24

*"Commit to the LORD whatever you do,
and your plans will succeed."*
Proverbs 16:3

*"May he give you the desire of your heart
and make all your plans succeed."*
Psalm 20:4

"For where your treasure is, there your heart will be also."
Matthew 6:21

*"Whatever you do, work at it with all your heart,
as working for the Lord, not for men."*
Colossians 3:23

4. *Consider Community:*

A Song of Ascents of David

*"How good and pleasant it is when brothers live
together in unity! It is like precious oil poured on the
head, running down on the beard, running down on
Aaron's beard, down upon the collar of his robes.
It is as if the dew of Hermon were falling on Mount Zion...For
there the LORD bestows his blessing, even life forevermore."*
Psalm 133:1–3

*"My prayer is not that you take them out of the
world but that you protect them from the evil one.
They are not of the world, even as I am not of it.
Sanctify them by the truth; your word is truth."*
John 17:15–17

The Following Passages are from Acts 2:41–47

*"Those who accepted his message were baptized, and about three
thousand were added to their number that day.*

The Fellowship of the Believers

*They devoted themselves to the apostles' teaching and to the fellowship,
to the breaking of bread and to prayer. Everyone was filled with awe,
and many wonders and miraculous signs were done by the apostles. All
the believers were together and had everything in common. Selling their
possessions and goods, they gave to anyone as he had need. Every day they
continued to meet together in the temple courts. They broke bread in
their homes and ate together with glad and sincere hearts, praising God
and enjoying the favor of all the people. And the Lord added to their
number daily those who were being saved."*

The Following Passages are from 1 Thessalonians 5:11–28

*Therefore encourage one another and build each other up, just as in fact
you are doing.*

Final Instructions

*Now we ask you, brothers, to respect those who work hard among you,
who are over you in the Lord and who admonish you. Hold them in
the highest regard in love because of their work. Live in peace with each*

other. And we urge you, brothers, warn those who are idle, encourage the timid, help the weak, be patient with everyone. Make sure that nobody pays back wrong for wrong, but always try to be kind to each other and to everyone else.

Be joyful always; pray continually; give thanks in all circumstances, for this is God's will for you in Christ Jesus. Do not put out the Spirit's fire; do not treat prophecies with contempt. Test everything. Hold on to the good. Avoid every kind of evil. May God himself, the God of peace, sanctify you through and through. May your whole spirit, soul and body be kept blameless at the coming of our Lord Jesus Christ. The one who calls you is faithful and he will do it. Brothers, pray for us. Greet all the brothers with a holy kiss. I charge you before the Lord to have this letter read to all the brothers. The grace of our Lord Jesus Christ be with you.

5. Consider Health:

"Worship the LORD your God, and his blessing will be on your food and water. I will take away sickness from among you."
Exodus 23:25

"My son, do not forget my teaching, but keep my commands in your heart, for they will prolong your life many years and bring you prosperity."

Proverbs 3:1–2

"(Further Benefits of Wisdom) Pleasant words are a honeycomb, sweet to the soul and healing to the bones."
Proverbs 16:24

"A truthful witness gives honest testimony, but a false
witness tells lies. Reckless words pierce like a sword,
but the tongue of the wise brings healing."
Proverbs 12:17–18

"But he was pierced for our transgressions, he was crushed
for our iniquities; the punishment that brought us peace
was upon him and by his wounds, we are healed."
Isaiah 53:5

...Your Mission Is Possible...

"The problem about destiny and the issue about
purpose is you cannot fulfill your destiny or find
your purpose unless you are connected to God."
Dr. Robert Scott

God Can Use Anyone from
Rahab to Rehab: The Remix
Abridged Version of Message Delivered at Central Baptist Church
by Reverend Dr. Robert Charles Scott, Pastor
Sunday, February 28, 2010

The scriptural reference for this sermon is found in Joshua 2:1–15.

An issue facing the church in general, and those who attend church specifically, is our reluctance to deal with how God can use those who we think are unworthy and unusable based upon what they do because we are not familiar with their story or how they got into their current situation. We tend to judge people based upon what we see and what they are doing, rather than looking beyond their faults and seeing their needs. There are many diamonds among us, but we miss seeing them sparkle because we would rather keep them buried than to let them shine.

The problem is made worse when a person does not have a relationship with God through Christ that will strengthen, sustain, and supply them. When you don't have a relationship with Christ, then you will never know what your purpose is and where you destiny will land you. A purpose filled with power and passion. A destiny provides a sense of direction to facilitate a move into the sovereign care of God. It is this destiny and purpose placing you within the reach of great blessings, demonstrating how awesome God is. God cannot use you if you are not aware of who He is. The problem about destiny and the issue about purpose is, you cannot fulfill your destiny or find your purpose unless you are connected to God.

The problem with many of us is that we are trying to do things without God. When you leave God out of the picture, you will discover many gaps that you cannot fill on your own. Regardless of credentials; regardless of finances; regardless of political affiliations; regardless of social connections, you and I cannot rise to the occasion unless we place our faith in God…I have to put my faith in God because the just shall live by faith. We have to put our faith in God because "without faith it is impossible to please God." We have to put our faith in God because that is how you and I got our salvation.

Let me press my claim to demonstrate the importance of faith in a rehab situation. I would not be where I am had not God saved me from my sins. In fact, because God saved me, I am in spiritual rehab. I am an ex-sinner saved by grace and every Sunday I show up, every time I come to Bible study, every time I have a devotional period with God, I am trying to be encouraged in my recovery efforts. The reason I have to be encouraged is that I have the propensity and proclivity for a relapse.

Every now and then, I fall short, and do something that makes God want to deny that He knows me. It is precisely why I try to make my way to the sanctuary Sunday after Sunday and get together with my fellow addicts and confess, "My name is Robert and I am a sinner saved by grace." Because at some time during the week, I had a relapse. I said something I should not have said. I thought something I should not have thought...That is why I have to do as David did and say to God, "Create in me a clean heart and renew a right spirit within me." Life has the tendency to catch you on a bad day and you will want to throw your religion out the window. Everyone has a need to get "straight" so that God may be pleased with our efforts and call us His own. That's what's happening in today's scripture.

The story of Rahab is connected to a reconnaissance mission, carried out by two spies into the land of Jericho. The Israelites were on their way to the land of Promise but standing before them was the fortified city of Jericho. Joshua sent two spies to find the weak links in the protection of city. It is interesting that these men of valor went to the house of a harlot, where they were able to find out the town's secrets...Rahab hid the spies from the citizens of Jericho because she had heard of these people, as being truly the people of God. She chose to be on the side and purpose of God. Because Rahab hid the spies, they gave their word that she and her family would be saved when the siege of Jericho was over. They gave Rahab a scarlet thread, telling her to put the bright red cord in the window of her house so that when the armies of the Lord passed through, they would protect the house...

We have all heard about high profile persons and their rehab situations linked to an alcohol, drugs, and sex addictions. When a person has to go into rehab, it is because their life is so out of control that intervention is necessary just for them to live and see another day. This is because their compulsion becomes the main factor in their life. They feel like they can't do without it. When you are caught in an addiction, you cannot pursue your purpose. This is because your addiction is your god that is keeping you captive, rather than Jesus who has come to set you free.

For Rahab and for us, sin is that compulsion that becomes the modus operandi of our reality. Even though I am saved and sanctified, I will admit that it is a struggle trying to do the right thing sometimes. That's what Paul meant when he said, "When I desire to do good, evil is present on every hand." And I am in rehab right now—not for a drug addiction; not for a sexual addiction; not for alcoholism; not for co-dependency. I am in rehab for sin addiction. *I know I'm saved but I still make mistakes. I know God has his hands on me, but there are times that, if He had not, I don't know what I might have done. I know God is doing a new thing in my life, but there are some days when the things I used to do make me want to go back…*

Can anyone relate to what I am saying? Perhaps you were on your way to the place where the summers are perpetual, and there is no air conditioner but God saved you. Why? Because He has a purpose for your life. He has a destiny designed just for you. That is why you are still alive. God is not finished with you.

This is why we are in spiritual rehab because every now and then when we have a relapse and fall, God, my counselor; God, my psychotherapist, tells me to get back up and to try it again because there is something for me to do. We are too valuable to Him for the sake of the kingdom. And if God can save Rahab and move, her to rehab, then God can do the same for you. What happens when a person moves from a place of sin to the position of spiritual rehab?

In order to experience spiritual rehab so that you can function in your purpose, you've got to put your faith totally in God. This is what Rahab did in the text. Rahab believed that God was going to give the Israelites the city of Jericho. Rahab turns from her former life and embraces the God of Israel. This is because she had heard about what God had done before and she believed he was the God of power. The city of Jericho was gripped by fear because they too, had heard about this God. They had heard…how God freed Israel from bondage in Egypt; how He parted the Red Sea; how God kept them in the wilderness and fed them manna in the morning and quail in the evening; and how God gave them victory over the Amorites. Therefore, because Rahab had heard…she got to a point where she believed. Romans 10:17 says, *Faith comes by hearing and hearing by the word of God.* She had not witnessed anything, she just heard. Jericho was in an uproar because they too, had heard. However, instead of them having faith, they trembled in fear. Yet, Rahab put her trust in the God who cannot fail.

I wonder how many people really have faith this morning. The only way I can keep my mind is because I have faith. When we are dealing with economic uncertainty, political confusion, war, senseless violence, and a declining job market, I've got to have faith. Faith has the tendency to contradict the facts. Facts say certain things – but faith says different…*I don't know how I'm going to pay my bills…God shall supply all your needs according to his riches in glory…I've got a disease that can't be cured…by His stripes I can claim my healing. I've got faith but nothing is happening…but faith without works is dead…I have done some things that are so out there that no one wants anything to do with me…if you confess your sins, He is faithful and just wants to forgive your sins and cleanse you from all unrighteousness.*

I have to walk by faith. I have to talk by faith. I have to give by faith. I have to live by faith. I have to love by faith. I have to shout by faith. I have to pray by faith. I have to praise by faith.

Next, the purpose God has for me is not predicated on what has happened in my past or what is going on right now, but my willingness to surrender to change for divine improvement in the future. So when I get into rehab, I cannot be judged by my activity, but by my identity. In other words, how I am identified is not by what I have done, but to whom I belong. In the text, after she has made this alliance with God and Israel, Rahab is no longer referred to as a harlot…She is a woman who took a risk to assist the people of God and in return, is rescued when the fighting begins…The implication is that Rahab is no longer considered a foreigner, that she belongs to the nation of Israel. And since she belongs to the nation of Israel, she belongs to God.

When you act on your faith, God will move on your behalf because you belong to Him. Salvation is never without conditions. You can't be saved without some conditions because God does not force Himself on anyone…You don't have to be defined by the circumstances you have created if you are connected to God. If you have done some things that, you are ashamed of, God knows what you have done, and He will forgive you.

When you come to God correctly, I'm talking about being committed and connected, you are then identified, and not by what you have done.…but as a child of His. Because God does not see you, the way people see you. God sees you as a son or daughter…because of the cross and the blood of Jesus. *What can wash away my sins? Nothing but the blood of Jesus. What can make me whole again? Nothing but the blood of Jesus.*

Finally, your negative current reality does not have to determine your future destiny. In other words, no matter how bad it is right now, your current situation does not have to have the last word. Rahab could have remained a harlot and been killed. However, in one moment, she decided to connect with God and her whole destiny was changed. By aligning with God, we call her name today—in a different light…

It is not until the New Testament, in first book of the Gospels, where we see the name Rahab again—she became the great-great grandmother of David, which means that she is in the lineage, or the bloodline of Jesus!

It does not matter how negative your situation may be, God can step in and make it work out for your *good*. A scarlet thread saved Rahab. There is another scarlet thread that protects our souls when the storms of life come. Christ is the scarlet thread to whom we have the blessed assurance that it is well with our soul. <u>**Jesus is**</u> the scarlet thread; the sinner's perfect plea; the seeker's end of the search; the saint's everlasting rest; a hiding place when the storms are raging; a bridge over troubled waters. Christ is the One who gives us safety and security when enemies harass us, when friends fail us, and when no one stands up for us. He is my scarlet thread.

It does not matter where you are right now. It does not matter how dark it is right now. It does not matter what people are saying about you—we serve a God who can change your situation around and He will carry you through. If God can rehab Rahab, then God can do the same for you…*If you can use anything Lord, You can use me. Take my hands Lord and my feet. Touch my heart Lord, speak through me. If You can use anything Lord, You can use me.*

I need God to wash me…make me brand new…give me new life…create in me a clean heart…renew a right spirit…refresh me…revitalize me…rekindle me…regenerate me…reaffirm me… reassemble me…retain me…reawaken me…reignite me…reseal me…rewire me…REHAB ME!!!

Dr. Robert Charles Scott is Pastor of Central Baptist Church in St. Louis, Missouri. To learn more about Pastor Scott, or to experience one of his sermons in person, please visit www.cbcstl.org.

Your Purpose, Your Destiny, and Your Legacy are
meant to be fully experienced and shared—
Leading you to a life of Extraordinary Living. It is Possible.

*And Jesus looking upon them saith, "With
men it is impossible, but not with God:
for with God all things are possible."*
Mark 9:27

…Your Mission Is Possible… Promise Yourself through the Messages You Send

The messages you send to yourself, through your thoughts and feelings are the ones, which will have the most impact on your future because your thoughts and feelings affect every aspect of your life. Finding reading material, which helps you to feel good about you and your life, is crucial to *Extraordinary Living in Action!*

The Optimists, a long-standing organization, and their members are committed to Optimism for themselves and for people around the world. Below, we share their adopted creed with you. The statement has a huge impact—if it is read, re-read, and possibly even memorized—that will remind you to live in a way becoming to the person you *really* are—*Extraordinary!*

The Optimist's Creed
(Written by Christian D. Larson—almost 100 years ago)

The Optimist Creed: Promise Yourself

> To be so strong that nothing can disturb your piece of mind.

> To talk health, happiness, and prosperity to every person you meet.

> To make your friends feel that there is something in them.

> To look on the sunny side of everything and make your optimism come true.

> To think only of the best, to work only for the best and to expect only the best.

> To be just as enthusiastic about the success of others as you are about your own.

> To forget the mistakes of the past and to press on to the greater achievements of the future.

> To wear a cheerful countenance at all times and to have a smile ready for every living creature you meet.

To give so much time to the improvement of yourself that you have no time to criticize others.

To be too large for worry, too noble for anger, too strong for fear, and too happy to permit the presence of trouble.

To think well of yourself, and to proclaim this fact to the world—not in loud words but in great deeds.

To live in the faith that the world is on your side so long as you are true to the best that is in you.

The Optimist Creed was authored in 1912 by Christian D. Larson, appearing in his book, *Your Forces and How to Use Them.* It was adopted as Optimist International's creed in 1922. Many have found inspiration in The Optimist Creed. In hospitals, the creed has been used to help patients recover from illness. In locker rooms, coaches have used it to motivate their players. [Squidoo.com]

...Your Mission Is Possible... Practical Planning and Stability during Your Mission

Simple Things I Really Want People to Know about Banking/Finance
Michelle Brown
Banker and Financial Planner

Michelle Brown Shares:
"Here are some financial tips for life:

1. Simply...'Save some money.'

2. Know your financial standing. Know how much money you have coming in versus going out—because it can be very costly when you spend more than you have. It will result in expensive fees, which can be astronomical over the course of a year.

3. Invest in property or real estate. It's always better to own, financially speaking. When you own your own home, you are making yourself richer. When you are renting, you are making someone else richer.

4. As parents and grandparents, open some type of savings vehicles like a 529 Savings Account for the children and ample retirement plans for yourself, such as an IRA (Individual Retirement Account). Have a plan that covers

various stages and kinds of expenses of your family life, it's important to have some type of long-term savings for your future.

5. Perhaps look into working for yourself—owning your own business—because if you pick the right business for your skill set, the payoffs can be great. Besides, a business is a great tax shelter, and you get to run the show."

About Credit Scores:

"Understand credit in general. Know your financial standing. It determines what you will pay for everything forever. People with poor credit are typically poor economically, but they end up paying the majority of costs for everything. Good credit is right up there with savings—paying bills on time and "keeping it together." When your credit is shot, it's hard to recover, and it is extremely important in terms of getting the best prices. Just think. In comparison, a person with poor credit could pay 20% versus the 2% for some things that the person with good credit pays."

Advice to Parents about Finances:

"Regarding money and your children, start them very early with their own savings account. Tell them, from every dollar they have to *save something*. Teach them: "save, give, spend." That works very well. It teaches them to be personally and socially responsible. In giving, tithing in the church or donating to a good group—a charity— works well. Teach children to save some money and take only a little portion to spend. That's real life, how it should and does work."

"You can teach children early with small amounts of money, such as $5.00–$6.00. Have them think in terms of percentages for savings and tithing, such as .50 for tithing—based on $5.00. Help them understand why they should support a charity and how much is reasonable to give, when they think about their own life as compared to that of others in need."

"Habits are established early when the grandparents, then parents, then children are "saving, giving and spending." You are instilling habits for children that they will take with them throughout adulthood. Train them to put money in the piggy bank. Model the behavior in the way you address the family budget and set priorities in your own spending. Soon, it will become second nature."

Michelle Brown is a mother of four and was a stay at home mom for many years. Michelle now manages a Fifth Third Bank Financial Center, where her primary focus is on educating the community about finances. Email: Michelle.Brown@53.com. For more information about savings plans, banking, or other financial planning visit www.53.com. Fifth Third Bank, Equal Housing Lender member FDIC.

…Your Mission Is Possible…
…Edifying the Spirit with Psalms…

Psalms for Practicing Christian Living-
New International Version

"Psalm 1 Gives Direction on How to Walk with the Lord"
Dr. Lee Roy Jefferson

Psalm 1
Two Ways of Life Contrasted

Blessed is the man
who does not walk in the counsel of the wicked
or stand in the way of sinners
or sit in the seat of mockers.
But his delight is in the law of the LORD,
and on his law he meditates day and night.
He is like a tree planted by streams of water,
which yields its fruit in season
and whose leaf does not wither.
Whatever he does prospers.
Not so the wicked!
They are like chaff
that the wind blows away.
Therefore the wicked will not stand in the judgment,
nor sinners in the assembly of the righteous.
For the LORD watches over the way of the righteous,
but the way of the wicked will perish.

"Psalm 23 is the language of being guided by the
Lord—the idea is that I need something above me,
outside of me, bigger than me to guide me."
Dr. Lee Roy Jefferson

Psalm 23
A Psalm of David.

The LORD is my shepherd, I shall not be in want.

He makes me lie down in green pastures,
he leads me beside quiet waters,

he restores my soul.
He guides me in paths of righteousness
for his name's sake.

Even though I walk
through the valley of the shadow of death,
I will fear no evil,
for you are with me;
your rod and your staff,
they comfort me.

You prepare a table before me
in the presence of my enemies.
You anoint my head with oil;
my cup overflows.

Surely goodness and love will follow me
all the days of my life,
and I will dwell in the house of the LORD forever.

"*Psalm 100 reminds us to be grateful*
for His blessings and mercy"
Dr. Lee Roy Jefferson

Psalm 100
A psalm. For giving thanks.

Shout for joy to the LORD, all the earth.

Worship the LORD with gladness
come before him with joyful songs.

Know that the LORD is God.
It is he who made us, and we are his;
we are his people, the sheep of his pasture.

Enter his gates with thanksgiving
and his courts with praise;
give thanks to him and praise his name.

For the LORD is good and his love endures forever;
his faithfulness continues through all generations.

Chapter 19

My Life and More
Dr. Lee Roy Jefferson

…That red tie…working on a sermon…my legacy
Survival of a Shipwreck

Acts 27:22—When Paul was going to Rome, the ship came into a storm. That night the Holy Spirit said, "You will lose the ship, but you won't lose your life. Your Salvation rests on holding on to a broken splinter of the ship…." Living on a broken splinter: positions that have gone awry, bad relationships, poor investments of time, talent, and life—those kinds of things. That's where hope is; that's where salvation is. Sometimes when things happen in life, we just need to find that splinter, and that's how we'll make it!

I'm "on call" for preaching—many call me at the last minute, and providing leadership at Northern Baptist School of Religion—while currently teaching a leadership class—I've decided I'm going to give my time…I'm on call.

While I was in New York in the '70's, Operation Bread Basket protested A&P under Rev William Jones. There were protests on Saturdays, along with planning meetings in the basement; then, it was come back to church on Sunday for worship—and that church seats 2,500 people. We were on Lexington & 53rd where the A&P headquarters were located, and we were on the bottom, trying to get up to the top. We were arrested before we could get to the top.

248

In Manhattan, I was arrested for civil disobedience and in jail from 6:00 pm-12:00 midnight (freed after six hours)—and met Rev Ralph Abernathy—he saw how shaken I was by being in jail and spoke to Marvin McMickle and advised him to put his arm around me so I wouldn't be uneasy…and to encourage me, and then he invited me to come and preach at his church. Two months later, I preached at West Hunter Street Baptist Church in Atlanta, Georgia, and that came out of that experience.

I told my friend, "Don't ever tell my mother that I went to jail. It would take her out of this world."

Reverend John Scott's Revelation at the Acropolis (How I met My Wife)

Reverend John Scott, who was a mutual friend, introduced my wife and me over the telephone. I was in seminary and the associate minister at Bethany Baptist Church in Brooklyn, New York, under the pastor, the Late Dr. William Augustus Jones, Jr., who was a noted Civil Rights leader and my beloved mentor.

Dr. Jones had a trip every year to the Holy Land with a delegation of about 40 people from the congregation, and, in April of 1972, I was a part of that delegation. Reverend John Scott, the Pastor of St. John Baptist Church in Harlem, had been a previous associate minister at Bethany and was my roommate on this trip. On our return from the Holy Land, we stopped in Athens, Greece. While walking up the Acropolis, I was ahead of him, and, all of a sudden, he shouted in a loud voice. When I turned to find out what was wrong, he said that he had a revelation on who was going to be my wife…. I said, "The air is too light. You need to sit down."

Within a week of our return, he introduced me to Jeanette Beckett (Jefferson) over the telephone, and we met within the week after that introduction...July 12, 1972. We dated from April 1972 until our wedding date, August 25, 1973, at Chapel at 120 & Broad Street in New York City.

When we dated, I would shine my shoes so much that you could look down and see yourself—that was my style. The only thing I regret is that I did not save that red tie I was wearing when I met her—because I tell her all the time that the red tie is what put her into a trance!

While I will mention my mentor, Dr. William Jones a few times, I want you to know that he passed around February 2006; and Reverend Jasper Payton served as the interim Pastor after Dr Jones became ill. He was recommended, because of his faithfulness and loyalty to Dr. Jones, he never did anything to undermine or underestimate him in terms of his leadership.

Defining Years, 1969–1972

Dr. Lawrence Jones (Dean/Professor; no relation to Dr. Wm. Jones) was the Dean of Union Theological Seminary in New York City at 120th & Broad Street. To picture the setting...all across the street was surrounding Barnard College, and on the other side was Columbia University Teachers College. On the corner was the Jewish Theological Seminary, with Manhattan School of Music, and behind the Seminary was Riverside Church. You could be inside the Seminary all week and not go outside because the basic needs were all there: school, housing, bookstore, housing, eating. We had a beautiful setting, the courtyard of the seminar, the picture where you get the green beautiful vines in August...

And he married us, Jeanette and me. I had a close bond with him, Dr. Lawrence Jones. As a student, I had grown close to him in terms of talking with him, listening to him, discussing issues, things of church, things of community. Even though he had his own department, as a faculty member, he would eat lunch in the cafeteria, which is how our relationship was nurtured. He's still alive and now lives in Silver Spring, Maryland; he was a dean for 20 years at Howard University… they just named the library after him.

Our Children

There is value in "foundation," having discipline as you live even at a young age. In preparation for the years to come, there is dedication to education, obedience to parents, loyalty to ideals, respect for traits of true manhood and womanhood, and traditions passed on to you from all who care; and, there is, of course, faith in God. Thus, my guardianship started for all those things as I *built* my adult life.

Daughter: I went to Bishop College in Dallas, Texas, and both our children would have attended there; however, it closed by the time Erica was ready to attend. So she took a loan to go to Hampton University with Business Administration as her major. My daughter, Erica Diane Jefferson-Gamble, has two boys. My grandsons are Christopher, age seven, and Isaiah, age five. Her husband is Robert Gamble, Jr., and they live in Brown Mills, NJ. Erica is Administrative Assistant for TD Banks. When they hire staff, it's through her department. Formerly, she worked at Rutgers.

Son: Byron Lee Jefferson is my son. His wife is Jeanelle. From their union has come my grandson Byron Lee Jefferson, II. He is three years old. They live in Bowie, Maryland, and he is a resident director with a staff of about twelve people working under his supervision at Bowie State University. He has been there for about four years now.

Bowie will soon be the University of Maryland at Bowie and a part of the whole University of Maryland Complex. Byron went to Cain University in New Jersey. He discovered while a resident director at the University of Maryland Eastern Shore that the job of resident director entitled the student worker to free tuition. A smart guy, he found out what to do to qualify and did just that; thus, he was able to finish school without paying tuition. I told him, at the time, that he needed to stay there because, as long as you are there, you pay no utilities, no rent. He is in a position to help himself *build* his life.

Family Foundation: The Results of Building and Preparing
I am number 7 of 5 Boys and 2 Girls.

Barbara, my oldest sister, attended Prairie View. In 1959, we became victims of polio. God healed me; however, she had to use a brace on her left leg, but she went on to graduate from Prairie View (now, A&M University) with a Bachelor's and Master's Degree. She served as Administrative Assistant to four college presidents there for 40 years and retired in 2003. My sister died 30 days after my mother in February 2008.

Brother Joe (Joseph Jefferson), who lives in San Jose, is a retired school teacher/graphic designer. He could draw and print, just take a pen and start.

Brother Isaac is in Houston, Texas. He went to the military and went into his own business. It entails making bids on property, lawn service, and land cleaning and clearing, and building demolition. He is doing very well. His son, an engineer, is now helping his father in the business.

Brother Delbert lives in Missouri City, Texas. He, too, is a minister who came into the ministry about 15 years after me. At one time, he was an appraiser for the federal government. Now, he is retired from his "job" and has a church in Houston, Texas. For the last 20 years, I have been his mentor.

Waverly, Jr. is an agricultural agent, but he retired about ten years ago. In the counties in Texas, people are serious about growing vegetables and various plants, as well as raising prize-winning animals. He is very involved in workshops and institutes. Every year, the county fairs, with their awards and prizes, occupy his time, especially in February when he participates in the Houston livestock show in February. As a son, he was the primary care provider.

Alma Dean Jefferson Smith (husband Jim, deceased) lives in Houston; and, courageously, she has raised three daughters and has been a childcare provider.

…And I have a green thumb, anything I plant is supposed to grow. The 7th child…it is a blessing to be the 7th child in the family.

Acquaintances and Building Foundations: I'd Like to Acknowledge…

I am a member of Metropolitan Baptist Church in Newark, New Jersey, where Dr. David Jefferson is Pastor and "builders" are preparing the way.

Mrs. Pansy King—She is the Director of Christian Education at Metropolitan; she is the one who recommended that I become a 2nd Vice President, then President of the General Baptist Congress of Christian Education for the State of New Jersey. Thanks to Pansy, I served in that capacity of the organization for a 12-year tenure, which resulted in my personal development, acquaintance with Christian educators and ministers in New Jersey, and my purpose to enhance Christian Education.

Dr. David Jefferson—I visited churches and was lead to become a member of Metropolitan. I wanted to go to a church where I would receive a positive message about the Word of God. I did not want to attend a church where people were in turmoil, conflict, "fussing at and with one another." The pastor does an excellent job in delivering a message. I am grateful that he has been a faithful minister in preaching the Gospel and exalting Christ in Worship. He has grown our church to three services, and a significant number of people are served as Metropolitan impacts the community. The church meets the needs and supports children in securing an education. An example is our "Back to School Project," through which we have given out 5,000 bags of school supplies for students! We have members who provide counseling to area residents every Tuesday. In efforts to serve the community, we appealed to area stores, which resulted in Marshall's® supporting our "5,000 Coat Give Away". Target® and others are also helping us to meet vital needs in the community. Because members are generating support for others, blessings are paying for the building.

Dr. George Waddles, Sr.—Pastor of Zion Hill Missionary Baptist Church, Chicago, Illinois. He ended his term as the Dean of the National Baptist Congress, and recently became President of the National Baptist Convention, Congress of Christian Education. He continues to positively impact people throughout the United States with his commendable and considerable commitment to Christian Education and to promoting the teachings of Gospel of Jesus Christ. Thank you for blessing us to also be the foreword writer for this book, as well.

George Wallace—He is a student at New Jersey Northern Baptist School of Religion and has been in several classes over the past few years. Employed as a law enforcement officer, he's a great guy, and has a great spirit.

I'm so pleased that **Deacon James Clark** succeeded me as President of the Congress. He is a terrific guy; he's fair, honest, and straight to the point, "what you call a straight shooter." He likes structure, order, integrity, honesty…just a good Christian person…all characteristic of "builders." He works with people, he teaches lay people, and he asks if he can come and just speak with them, a volunteer.

Dr. Warren Steward—He is the Pastor at First Institutional in Phoenix, AZ. We both went to Bishop College, and he was chair of the Home Mission Board of the National Baptist Convention, which provide leadership of churches in the United States. This is important because this is part of our mandates as Christians and Baptists, doing our missionary work.

Dr. William Shaw—I have lived in his house. Once when I went to revival, closing was so late that he invited me to stay at his home. What a Blessing it was that he showed me hospitality, encouragement, and ministerial support!

Dr. Geoffrey Guns—Pastor of Calvary Baptist Church, in Norfolk, Virginia. He's also a teacher in the National Baptist Congress. Dr. Guns teaches through lecture presentations. He has done so for years. He is a good teacher, writer, and preacher. A year ago, he baptized 350 people at one time. The candidates were people who joined the church within a 30-day period. Let's make it clear. That was after they had received teaching and training to prepare them for their Christian walk with the Lord. It's quite exciting!

Thank you all…humbly from my heart.

THANK YOU, GOD…I obtained my first Degree from Bishop College; I received mentorship from **Dr. E. V. Hill**; and **Mr. Hogan** was placed directly in my path when I arrived on campus.

Chapter 20

Thank God for My Unique Blend of Family, Friends, and Mentors
Jo Lena Johnson

What children sometimes need is a parent to notice when things go haywire!

As a young person, around 4th grade or so, I was "sent" to counseling-time that I had with my very own "Dr. Skiddis" (I'm not sure if that's the correct spelling of her name) as I often completed my work quicker than other students and would then begin to talk (distracting them from finishing). I remember treasuring those times because she would give me little projects to do. I felt productive and comfortable with her. I don't know what my parents told me (at the time, my household included my mom, my dad, William McHugh, Sr., and my younger brother, William, Jr.). I feel the need to explain a couple of things to you—so that you will get the context of what I have and haven't said, thus far.

Parents

When I was very young, I remember days when my mom, Sandra (Sandy Johnson) McHugh, and I would be standing in the checkout line, and I would read the little books—I just always knew there was more to know, and I wanted access to the information. Does anyone remember the "Farmer's Almanac" or the "Reader's Digest" or the little horoscope books that would be right there? Well, those things gave me insight that there *was* more to learn than just what was in school. But, first things first…

There are two people who "brought me forth"—Sandra and Kenneth Johnson. When I was around two years old, my young parents, decided to get divorced. They had dated for years, ever since high school when my mom was a young "track star" in Des Moines, Iowa, and my father was a young "football star." These two people were…are bright, smart and, back then, they were involved in many activities. When they were in high school, they were active and engaged in learning, sharing, and athletics. However, it was the late 60's, and when the Viet Nam War called, young Kenneth Johnson became a soldier.

Since my mom was two years younger, and still in high school, they did their best to "stay together;" and, they eventually married after my father "returned from the war." Yet, so many things happened in both their lives during that period of separation. Though I have yet to confirm it, I suspect that their level of comfort with each other and their mutual vibrancy, similar family values, and common interests played a huge role in why they chose to get married; but, evidently not enough to sustain them after the war and social upheaval of the 60's.

Well, one thing we do know is that I needed to be born so, "Voilá"— you are reading this book! Yet, at the ages of 19 and 21, I'm not sure that those two young people knew the responsibilities and hardships that they would face, when coming together to live in the same quarters and to set priorities. When I was born, they were 21 and 23, and I believe they separated sometime between my 2nd and 3rd birthday. I don't think many people in my mother's life understood why a young mother would divorce her husband—a provider—with the responsibility of a small child back then. I also don't think many people understood what happened. They probably could not understand why a young father, who just returned from war, might find it difficult to adjust to being in a committed, structured, and fairly non-eventful home life.

I have so many mixed feelings about my parents' behavior. I love them so much. I appreciate them so much; yet, I get frustrated, even today, at 39 years old, at what they do and say sometimes. As a very little person, I remember, vaguely, trying to get them to stop yelling at each other. As a little person, I remember being in my mom's kitchen with her "giving me instructions" to give to my father, who was on the other end of that yellow corded kitchen phone, because they refused to speak to one another.

Yet, somehow, I was sent a "protector"...a just man who entered and transformed my life—and who cultivated my love of the law, justice, and balance. My "Dad"...William J. McHugh, Sr.

He was usually at work when the "former" Mr. and Mrs. Johnson were fighting through me. He was the person who taught me to sit up straight and to stay forward in the backseat while we were in the car—and I would be mad at him sometimes because I thought he was so strict. Yet, he would share stories of his days at his job when we were at the kitchen table. Early on, before he became a Judge for the St. Louis Municipal Courts, he worked at Juvenile Hall. Over dinner, the four of us (mom, dad, sister, and brother) would share the events of our day, over the table that I helped to set.

Folded napkin on the left, with fork on top; glass plate in the middle and knife—with ridges facing toward the plate—and spoons—if we needed them for that meal—to the right of the knife. The glass, usually a 12 ounce size, would be placed "above and to the right of" the knives, on the right side. My duties, along with setting the table, were to wash the dishes, complete homework, and be off the telephone and in the bed—all by 9pm. Those were the days! …I can say that now—but not then.

At the table, we would have just heard about what happens when children get into trouble, what happened with mom and her art clients; and, of course, I'm sure that they patiently listened to whatever I was "blabbing about" on that particular night or at that meal. I've always been a talker (that's why I'm writing volumes of books; I'm telling you now, so that I don't lose you).

Aunt Jerry

With Daddy McHugh came Aunt Jerry! She's his sister, and she's also a Leo (like me and Rev. Mac, and several of my favorite people). Aunt Jerry is the "role model" whom I think all kids deserve—an adult who loves them, cares for them, shares with them, teaches, and guides them, and who does not have to deal with all of the discipline and pressures of parenting. (I don't know when Aunt Jerry learned to cook; however, she prepares some of my most favorite foods when I visit her—including collard greens, turkey wings, and cabbage.)

I created a (soon to be available) youth book series titled *Aunt Jerry Loves Blue—and So Can You* because that woman showed me that I could travel, write, be nice, and have fun while helping people. She taught me this because that's been her life. She modeled the lesson; she did it by living it. She has always liked fancy, girly things, the latest trends, and color. The woman used to be a "plus sized model" and I think she should be the "mature face" of Ashley Stewart right now! She's Fluffy, She's Fancy, and She's Fun! You can read more about her real life adventures—she has plenty, living in the Washington, D.C.

metro area. Yet, I want to be specific about why every child should have an "Aunt Jerry."

Aunt Jerry sent cards for every occasion—St. Patrick's Day, Easter, Halloween, Thanksgiving…and "she" was usually the real gift at Christmas because she would come back to St. Louis to visit us! One year, I think it was about 1984, she took my brother, and I to Northwest Plaza in St. Louis (called a plaza because the stores were not attached and one had to walk outside in order to get to the next store). It was so cold that the locks on the car door were frozen. It was so cold, and although she vaguely remembers it, but we (big-little people always remember such things) remember being so cold and being with her. That was enough for us. With Aunt Jerry, we found loving tenderness and fun-loving guidance. She cared for us; groomed us; and she still does, by writing letters and by showing us historic monuments—in person and vicariously through the "novel" (letters) that she's sent throughout the years. I have a box of them right now—I just need to find it!

Aunt Jerry listens and she is empathetic. She has been a member of her church, St. Joseph's Catholic Church, for over 30 years. Even as she neared retirement, she continued to donate to the Firemen, the Policemen, and many entities under the United Way. She has always spoken up for people. In the 1980's my Aunt Jerry became the first black female from her district to be sworn in as a Delegate for the State of Maryland. As a result, she helped to shape laws that still affect citizens of the state today. After serving her term in office, she went on to work for the Governor's Office and then to spend many crucial years as an advocate for children while working with the Maryland Infants and Toddlers Program.

As a wife, she loved her mate, although her marriage to Uncle Leon lasted only five years (he died of complications due to diabetes). He became more than "fluffy," because of his diet of rich foods; but he gave my Aunt a number of years of entertainment and pleasure as her #1 supporter. She allowed him to "lead her to victory" in the campaign, and to build the courage and confidence to leave her hometown of St. Louis, and to make a positive impact on her nieces, nephews, and children around the world. She listened to him; he loved her. He was assertive and sometimes loud. She was sweet, appropriately reserved, and always appreciated for her contributions.

Aunt Jerry travels to Israel and beyond. She loves her dog Blue, and I do too. I'm much more comfortable with this little Bijon' Frise' than I was with Napoleon, an oversized German Shepherd who scared the day lights out of me with his "friendly" self when I was smaller than he was.

Aunt Jerry is active in her community: She is enrolled as a "Senior Citizen Student" in Prince George's Community College; she swims; goes to Curves; enjoys the Amish Market and her mini (purple) Dell™ laptop; and she frequently goes places with her good friend, Lorraine. She's supportive. It would take too long to share all of the ways; so, just know that when I needed a "home" and needed to be with family, she opened hers to me. I'm realizing now, more than ever, that it's not easy living with someone like me—who is "so fast." She's just wonderful!

So…thanks Daddy, for marrying my mom, so that I could have you, Mom, and Aunt Jerry.

I know this was a lot, but, hopefully, you see how relationships, family, and communication—especially in families—can and do influence the lives of children.

The Transitional Years—I'm still not where I'm going but,
I'm no longer in the City of Angeles.

Rev. Mac

The transition started when I lost my "Spiritual Mother," Reverend Delores Francine McMillan on April 10, 2002. She had taught me so many things I needed to know, and many that I didn't have a clue that I needed to know. I'll share more about her as we go along…

I miss her so much. She loved me unconditionally, and she taught me how to read the Bible; how to slow down and pay attention to people and their individual needs; and how to get beyond the desire to "know and understand" everything. I used to think I needed to know it all. I often used to say the phrase, "I know" a lot. Rev. Mac told me to stop saying that. She also told me to eat peppermint because it would "keep me sweet." In other words, "Girl, your mouth is getting you in trouble again! Your lack of patience is inappropriate, so take a chill!" Those are just some of the things she taught me.

I've lost friends, co-workers, bosses, and customers along the way because of my big mouth and being too direct and straightforward about things. I am a "work in progress." Therefore, if you meet me and I seem focused, I'm probably getting ready to do something *really* important, or I just finished doing something *really* important. I may not notice or have the capability, in that moment, to know what you want or need. If you are patient with me, I promise you I will respond accordingly. And…sometimes, it takes me a while to "get stuff." You know…understand. Some people call it "hard headed."

That's part of the beauty of Rev. Mac's and my relationship! I would come up with a bright idea and I would tell her in detail what was happening, why it was happening, and what I planned to do about it! Then, she would be very open, honest, and direct with me. She would help me reason through the pros and the cons, the risks and rewards, and the causes and effects of what I was up to. In addition, let me tell you, when my bright ideas involved dating, I was clever. Not in a negative way, I was just a sucker for well-dressed, clean-cut, and intelligent men who were productive and acted graciously toward me. The problem was that *they weren't for me.* When "those" types of ideas came up, I would share, and she would listen. Then, she would say, "Leave it alone. Leave it all the way alone!" And, you know what? Nine out of ten times I would...but, that one time, that one bright idea (every tenth; you know, I've always been productive) would be that time when I would "learn the hard way."

Reverend Mac had plenty of opportunities to say, "I told you so," and she never did. She comforted me through the mistakes, the pain, and the poor choices. She just loved me.

This relationship did not negate my relationship with my mom. No one can or will replace the love that exists between my mother Sandy McHugh, and me. It's just that sometimes, one needs a clean slate and a fresh start...and when growing up with people, sometimes we "hold them" to past behavior. Being my mom during my junior high/high school years was not easy. The love, concern, compassion, and attention she has given to me throughout—in addition to birthing me—clearly, nothing can replace. And, the closer we are to people, sometimes we are not able to recognize or acknowledge growth, development, or maturity.

When I met Rev. Mac, I was a few days older than 26. I lived in Los Angeles and had been going through a divorce. I had lost over 40 pounds of weight that I picked up during college and during a stressful marriage. I went to church that day because something inside me knew that I needed help—that I needed guidance and that I needed love. Although Rev. Mac never bore children, she had "grown folks" that she mothered, like me.

Rev. Mac was wise and yet, she was still a woman. She was loving, yet stern; caring yet, fun; and she loved God— loved reading and teaching the Bible, and her "children." She loved the Lord, loved His Word, and she taught it with the full force of the whole Spirit of God energizing her being.

After Rev. Mac passed, I went into a cloud of sorrow, hurt, pain, and a fight with the rental company to whom I had leased (for her) a nice home in Las Vegas. Because both our names were on the lease, even though she had passed, they would not allow me to get out of the lease. They said that I was still alive; therefore, I had to pay.

I was angry too. A young person should not have to bury an older person who does not have a life insurance policy or money to cover their final expenses—moving, burial, end of life, etc. Also, a young person should not have to call and beg people to help pay to put to rest the life, world, and affairs of someone who had spent a lifetime of serving and giving to others. There are at least 100 living teachers and preachers who directly benefited from the Bible Teaching of the Right Reverend Delores Francine McMillan; yet, when it was time to bury her, I can say that a sad few were there to help.

I didn't know what to do with a lifetime of treasures, but what I did know is that I would handle her business the way she had taught me—decently and in order. Yet, she didn't tell me that she was dying. That hurt. The day before she passed, she called me. We talked about everything. She asked me about my mom (we always talked about her), my brother, my business ventures, my close friends, and all kinds of other things. It was just the best conversation ever! One that led me to believe that we would enjoy each other's company on that following Sunday, when I would have completed my three events—one in honor of my friend, Allison Fisher who passed of breast cancer; a Stoli Vodka kick-off party that I managed, held at the Playboy Mansion/Hugh Hefner Estate; and the other, an Upscale Magazine re-launch event. It was one of those "crucial weeks" in my life…I told you I was productive.

She was doing what parents often do, trying to protect me from the seriousness of her illness by not telling me what was *really* happening. I had emotional, logistical, financial, and relational issues to deal with as a result. If I had known, I can't say what I would have done differently; however, I know I would have "been there." And, thus, that's why she didn't tell me. She did not want me to interrupt everything in my life—all those "career making" breakthroughs that one gets in "Hollywood" and that can set a person up for life.

But, I loved her, and though she prepared me in other ways for her loss, by not knowing her condition, I was left in a tough financial position. I was faced with commuting back and forth to Las Vegas from Los Angeles—a quick hour on Southwest Airlines, but a four-hour drive in my little black Honda. In order to sort through the literally hundreds of books, thousands of papers, and almost 50 boxes that were unpacked in her 2 car garage, it took resources, time and challenges which a few simple conversations could have prevented—or at least, made the tasks easier.

Notes to Parents Who Have Raised Responsible Children

1. Since you are aging, please take time to draft a will. It helps with communication, once you have found your rest. It will help those left behind to know how to handle your affairs.

2. When you are ill, short-term, or long-term, please inform your children about what is happening with your health. Even if they are really little, they know when you are not feeling well, but may not realize how much so…

3. When you are having financial problems and do not have life insurance, regular insurance, or enough income to pay for your medicines, please let somebody know— especially a young person who is strongly, daily connected to you. With the internet, it's much easier to at least, try to research remedies.

4. When you have young people who love you and they are out of town, please really consider what you share with them— and what you don't…it's not a good feeling to wonder if your loved one has enough bread or milk or is taking care.

5. When you are faced with a challenge and cannot take care of yourself in the manner that you are accustomed or need, please allow others to assist you. Assist you in a way that they can manage—not in a prideful-selfish way that makes them choose between continuing to work, raise their families, or move to where you are because you are unwilling to compromise.

6. When you need something, please be clear about what you need. Many of us want to assist you; however, make certain you need it, not just want it. In other words, those closest to us know how to "push our buttons." Therefore, please be fair to everyone.

If you're giving up your house to come support your children and grandchildren with your chipper presence, flexibility, family songs and stories, traditions, and the occasional "baby sitting duties," please do. These things are probably welcomed and requested. Go for it!

"What I now know about Kenneth 'Tough Love Daddy' Johnson"

> *"Stubborn, stern, strong, direct—that's the Dad I grew up knowing, and, many times, dreading."*
> Jo Lena Johnson

> As a daughter who occasionally encountered my father during summers, some holidays, and mostly by telephone—when we were actually speaking to one another—I really didn't understand my dad—and I KNEW he didn't understand me. For most of those 25 years, we would argue, disagree, get angry, not speak, and in general "act up" with each other. It was painful for me and I always wanted to please him & for him to be proud of me—but...
>
> He wouldn't change! He was the parent, after all...

Then I had an experience that helped me to look at him, and certainly myself differently. I attended a church service the first weekend of August, 1996; as a result of "wanting to be a better person," I committed several years of my life to learning & practicing the teachings at that church. They taught ways to read, study and interpret the Bible, which were not new—they were simply new to me. They explained forgiveness to me—and the importance of taking action when anyone or I wanted a new or different result. They made it practical and plain—and based on what I heard, I knew that I HAD to forgive my Dad. So, by Thanksgiving of 1996, I was ready, armed and willing to change our relationship. That was my attitude when I went to visit him. I wanted him to get to know me, see how sweet and kind I was, and I was determined to be flexible, harmonious, forgiving, and let whatever he said or did roll off my shoulders! We would have the BEST visit ever and our lives would be great from that visit on!

> *Do you think that, everything was easy after*
> *20+years of strife, just because*
> *I was ready for things to be different?*

Now, I have absolutely no recollection of what was happening in my Dad's life at that time. I'm not sure if he was married to my step-mom at that time, how his business was going, or what he was thinking or feeling about his own life. I just know I loved that man and I wanted things to be better. Looking back, it's a shame that I can't give you more details about HIM now. But, isn't that just like a child, or person? Self-focused!

I can tell you what was happening in my life. By the weekend of my 26th birthday in July 1996, I was fresh from a long-term relationship and subsequent divorce; bruised from "high stakes dating" of which I had no perspective—and no game; having gone to 2 counseling sessions; and knowing deep inside that there had to be more to life than how I was feeling, the counselor told me point blank: **go to church**. Eventually, after a few more poor choices and another bad 1st date, I went to church.

That church deserves a whole novel so I won't do it justice here but, I do need to share a few things about why it's important to my dad and myself....The day I entered the sanctuary was the day that my entire life changed. Of course, I believed in God, in Jesus and had been to church before. However, it was something about that day—from the moment I woke up that morning, I was nervous but not scared; unsure but determined, and I knew my willingness to go somewhere I had never been was the reason this is where I was supposed to be. I met people who would help shape my views, thoughts, and actions—and would give me some understanding of myself and others, which I had been missing.

During my time at Understanding Principles for Better Living Church, two very different women taught me some big life lessons, which helped lay the foundation for the Dad whom I was to discover. The first was Minister Della Reese, whose sermon that day was titled "My Claim to My Inheritance." In the moments that followed, though I had been crying already, I began crying rivers as I listened, learned, and was touched by something far greater than a person. From that Sunday on, Rev. Della as we call her, filled my experiences as she taught Christian Principles by preaching about practical things in her life, like cooking, choosing a mate, relationships of all kinds, love, dumb mistakes, experiences and miracles, all boiled up into one crock pot full of humorous Goodness.

The second was the Assistant Minister, Reverend Delores F. Mc Millan. I've shared about my experiences with Rev. Mac already however you need to know that she was *really* working with me. What to do and how to do certain things, about being a young woman, dating, marriage, and men—including my Dad!

By the way, that Thanksgiving trip ended up being pretty good—considering others, which had been disastrous. And no, it wasn't easy, and yes I messed up, and (of course) he messed up, but, hey it was a few days so, great! But, I still didn't feel totally safe with my

Dad. When I say "safe" it means that Rev. Mac could say just about the very same thing Dad said but, I would receive it a different way because of the history and patterns of our relationship. By that time, I'm sure he didn't know how to connect with me either, though I would never have thought or considered that then. It was the quality of the good times, and the context with which she would share things with me that helped me to listen to her—and to trust her.

My dad on the other hand, I always thought he was just tough, strong, had no feelings and just didn't like me—that I wasn't good enough for him. I'm not blaming him for my thoughts—I'm simply sharing them. I was trying forgiveness but, again, I really hadn't had a lot of guidance or practice in application. Looking back, I think if he had shared some of his stories with me, good ones, bad ones, times when he may have felt defeated or triumphant, I would have felt safer with him. But, as a man, growing up as a Baby Boomer, having served in Viet Nam, and trying to make it the world himself, I don't know if he even thought of this either. I know my Grandpa Johnson wasn't a "touchy feely" type of guy in general—though he did begin to soften by the time us grand children came around.

Forgiveness. I heard it, studied it, and was willing to try it—
but, I had no experience in it—and did not know how to do it

Making any principle a habit takes willingness, flexibility, determination, commitment and practice. There are some thoughts, ideas, concepts and behaviors that will NEVER be natural for me, for my dad, or for anyone. However, when one hears, learns and experiences—and is willing to take the lessons (good and bad), and try something new, skill building will result with focus and steadfastness. For example, if my Dad's parents had taught him to share his feelings freely by showing him theirs, or if he had someone in his life like a Rev Mac while maturing who could have taught him to "simmer down" like she painstakingly was trying to teach me, perhaps our experiences would have been different. Perhaps if my mother, had a different perspective of my Dad as a man, or had chosen to communicate her feelings differently about him to me while I was growing up; perhaps in our Father-Daughter relationship, we could have both felt Safer with each other.

However, it's not up to my Grandparents, Parents, Friends or even my Dad (for that matter) for me to get along better with him—it's my choice. Just like it's your Choice—what you see, hear, feel, think, and ultimately do. Stuck yes—choice always—willing to move—Maybe?

Reality Check.
It's Spring 2010, and after so many
years of practicing good habits,
things are perfect in my life, my dad's
life, and in our relationship!

The above statement is not true!!!

So many changes have happened in our lives. I still feel a way, think a way, and don't necessarily agree with my Dad about certain things. I can be serious, long winded, and analytical. I am also fun, a big kid at heart, and my mouth still gets me into trouble sometimes. I'm a natural entrepreneur and I love learning. I still want everybody to succeed, speak up, feel good, be healthy, and I'm a little unconventional. I feel honored to encounter people daily who show me ways to grow, stretch, and behave in better ways. I don't have as many answers as I used to think I did, and I'm in a state of transition at this very moment.

Yet, there is hope. There is Choice. It is possible to be fulfilled and to strive for more and different, if we are willing. I must be honest with you; I don't really know that my dad is "different." I can't say that he's "changed." What I can say is that through events, study, and willingness, my perspective has changed. I was incapable of seeing him a different way before. I will say this, that as many years as it has taken (and it's still hard sometimes) my experience and view of my Dad is different. *Would you care to meet him?*

Gregarious and focused, he is skilled in many things—including board and card games!

Kenneth Johnson is fun and he's super "cool" (it was KJ COOL before Obama Cool!) He's bright, handsome, has high-standards, pays attention to detail and appreciates quality. He is kind hearted, sincere, genuine, and has a strong desire to make a positive difference in the lives of those he touches. He has been, and continues to be a trusted, respected professional & business owner in the insurance industry. He is really active at church and likes to assist families during their time of grief at funerals.

He is a devoted husband to Vera. She is a blessing to the family because not only does she love, and understand him; she is patient and shows him how much she appreciates him.

My dad has shared wisdom that continues to stick with me—and I am honored and proud to know him, love him and like him. And the "good news" is he's alive and well and available for us to grow, continue to learn from, and love each other. It's not too late! I'm still not "easy"—and I probably never will be. However, I'm a work in progress and I know that my Dad loves me and he shows me, he shares with me, he still gives me tough love, and very recently, when there was a huge opportunity for conflict, instead of reverting to "what used to happen" the "safety zone" in our relationship is expanding through it.

As I write this, my dad may be speeding along in his souped up golf cart or nodding off to sleep in his chair in front of the TV. Wherever he is, and whatever he doing, I hope that in his heart and mind, he knows that I know what I know about Kenneth Johnson.

No Real Regrets!

At the same time, I don't really regret events or decisions I made because I have met some really good people along the way. People whom I fell in love with or who fell in love with me. There have been times when I met a person and they didn't like me, and I knew it. Depending on where we were, or what we were doing, or if I had a responsibility to them because they were in one of my classes or something, I would work really hard to connect with them. Then there were some I had no taste for, so I moved on. At other times, there were people who probably didn't care for me, my style, or for what I was "about," and I probably did not even have a clue!

It's amazing how many times I've been called "in love," how many cities I've traveled to, and how many ventures I have begun and ended. I just see *good* all over the place! It's been hard, with my little mind, to discern for which people, places, and things I should invest my time, talent, energy, and thoughts. I've been showered with more true friends than any one human being deserves!

I've driven through mountain passes (a fancy word that people in Washington state call a mountain road) in below freezing temperatures. I have driven through overflowing waters (rivers) in the Poconos. I have traveled to and through 48 states, four provinces in Canada, and over 21 cities in the United Kingdom without incident.

That is a miracle! God is good.

Along the way, I have offended, created discomfort, and spoken up a bit too much. Some days were really hot. Some days, like one in Syracuse, New York, was really cool. Yet I'm thrilled to think of the glorious opportunities I've had to meet, and share, and learn from so many *really* good people.

As I Sit Here Writing...

I have a renewed sense of freedom, bigger, and sweeter serenity.

I don't know how things will work out because, in each area of my life, I have lots of work to do; however, I do know beyond any doubt that I am destined to proclaim Truth around the world. The truth about God, the Holy Spirit, and Jesus in a way that people will get and receive it, according to my belief in Him who strengthens me.

Let me say that I believe *God is the good and very good.* I believe that He is everywhere, evenly, and equally present. I believe that He knows all. I believe He is all-powerful. I believe He loves us more than we are capable of conceiving. I happen to be a Christian. As a novice, but lifelong student of religion and other matters, I also believe that there are many holy texts, and instructions, and people that God has sent for the benefit of His children.

So, whatever your chosen religion or spiritual practice, I ask you to be open and willing to consider the things shared with you. My request is that you simply consider. I don't expect you to agree with everything, or even anything, I have to say. Yet, I do know that as you invest your time, thoughts, and feelings into the context of this literature, *good* is created in our universe. Good can come to us through words, as well as actions. Words in themselves can be glorifying, uplifting, blessings—or they can create wounds that are binding in thoughts, emotions, deeds, and in results.

Returning to the Initial Setting of the Message — Scenes from My Childhood

A Note to Parents: Caring for Children Physically, Mentally, and Emotionally

1. Children need their parents.

2. Children need hugs and love freely given.

3. Children also need to be given the space, the capacity, and the opportunity to learn, to question, and to be led with wisdom, guidance, and understanding.

4. When adults miss appointments with children; forget birthdays; forget meals; fail to check on homework; don't encourage; or don't share, even when tough things are happening in the home, children then make up things according to their own understanding.

5. When having financial problems, health problems, work problems, emotional problems and such, sometimes parents hold back, but children can *sense* things. They know there is "a problem." Do not ignore children, and don't keep them "out of the loop," hoping to "protect them" or "protect you." It is *not* acceptable to ignore them and it is detrimental to their successful upbringing; it is *not good*. Give even simple explanations, a little assurance, and some evidence of wise guidance. You will feel better, your children will feel better, and ultimately, you will create a healthier environment for your family.

P.S. This balance of this book is dedicated to the healing, which I'm praying to have. I love people, especially my people. And, no matter what they do or say, I will not stop loving them…and I do forgive them. However, not all behavior is acceptable—from them, from me, or from you.

As you consider what has been shared in this volume, if you have found anything acceptable, anything pleasing, anything worthy, please choose to practice it.

Praise God—and Thank you, for being willing!

Thank you, Friends, Family, Schoolmates, and Teachers for the "Living" Support!

"Pay Attention and listen to the sayings of the wise; apply your heart to what I teach, for it is pleasing when you keep them in your heart and have all of them ready on your lips."
Proverbs 22:17 (NIV)

Without the kindness, generosity, friendship, lessons, wisdom, and influence of the people below, I would be incapable of expressing myself and these volumes to you. Directly, and indirectly, each "Extraordinary" persons contributed to my experience, perspective, and, thus, my ability to share with you.

I am extremely grateful, and I thank God for each person. You have met many of my wise friends throughout this book; however, I have been extraordinarily blessed with people who have taught me, shared, guided, supported, and contributed to my living, and to thousands of people throughout the world.

I smile at the experiences when I was "really close" to a person or "really active" in a particular project or group. This volume would not be complete without thanking each person on this list. This is my effort to "tell the world" how great you "really" are!

Thank you for this book, Dr. Lee Roy Jefferson, Dr. George Waddles, Sr., and each person who contributed wisdom to this endeavor. Please continue your good works because we need you! A heartfelt hug to Vera J. Raglin—my teacher, my friend, and a brilliant example of dedication, commitment, loving-kindness, and integrity.

La Tia King, Pamela Williams, Deionci Walker, Lorraine Sebastian, Avis Laden, Jewel Wilkes, Erika Whitfield, Jessica Wesley, and Jennifer Armstrong, thank you for your friendship, support, encouragement, feedback, and enthusiasm during the writing and editing processes, and in my life's journey. You are beautiful gifts and inspiring souls.

Dr. Jody J. Squires, Kim Crouch, Dionne Peeples, Michael Wotorson, and Professor Clyde Ruffin—your tireless commitment to activism, to education, to youth, and to community have inspired me for over 20 years. I treasure you, and I thank you.

Lilbert Hollins and Family—thank you for your love, nurture, and the joy that we have shared. I thank God for the opportunity to know and love each of you.

Mentors/Teachers/Role Models/Friends: Flint Fowler and Terry Freeman, during my INROADS/St. Louis experience; Dr. KC Morrison, Professors Jean Allman, Geta Le Seur, and the late Paulette Grimes from University of Missouri (Mizzou); Teachers Jacqueline Edwards and Jerry Kottler; Friends: Denise Poindexter, Frederica Collins, Bill Freilane, Shawn Fields, Tina Grimes, James Hill, (Mr.)

Kim Love, Rachel Burse, and Charlotte Ottley—The people of St. Louis benefit so much by your presence.

Riverview Gardens High School Classmates, Friends, Best Friends, and Great People: Rosalind (Day) Lane, Denise (Campbell) Kayira, Bridget (King) McCord, Jewell (Johnson) Williams, Mia Smith, Antoinette Pearson, Yolanda (McGaughey) McGuire, Rhonda (Lingard) Willis, Pam (Blackmon) Crawford, Lynette (Coleman) Francis, James Buckley, and Eric Smith, Sr.

Cecil Parker (Class of 1987)—Thank you for being there to see me off at my Senior Prom, for providing your videotaping services now, and for sharing your humility, service, and talent through "formal church work" and beyond, your friendship and brotherhood are blessings to me.

Prayer Warriors: Vera S. Johnson, Eurita Farrelly-McLean, "Grand Mommy" Mable King— God uses you, and I'm so glad to be on your prayer lists. I love you all so much, and I'm so blessed to be loved by you.

I grew up just knowing that I was "meant" to be a woman of Delta Sigma Theta Sorority, Incorporated. Eventually, my dream was fulfilled (Epsilon Psi, Spring '91), and I am humbled and honored to our Founders for their vision, fortitude, and tenacity—especially at a time when women *really* needed it. I think we still *really* need sisterhood, and I'm grateful to my line sisters and other sorors who pave the way daily in service, commitment, and in creating the *extraordinary*. I want to particularly acknowledge Sorors: Jackie Swift, Aretha Jones, Tracy Thomas, Kimberly Presberry, Shante' Redden, Kelli Jordan, Sylvia Flowers, Shene' Redden, and Gayle Walker. You each showed me what sisterhood is, and is not. I love you.

Ruth Williams, Attorney James Nowogrocki, Debbie Fisher, Commissioner Greg Howard, Debbie Freisinger, Sue Anderson, Donna Gamache, Pam Ross, Tessa Greenspan, Jim Robbins, Jeff Gibbs, Carlos Calvo, Luis Da Silva, Dick Kaku, Rick Young, and Kathleen Christ of the St. Louis Aquatic Healing Center— Each of you has been instrumental in my professional growth, development, and sometimes my sanity. I *really* appreciate you.

Living in Los Angeles was an important and necessary part of my life—I miss it and I treasure the people, places, things, and experiences. It was a place of learning, growth, and developing lifelong friends. We had fun too. I thank God for the "safety" of having friends from college/St. Louis come together to "make it" together—Chris Davis, Steve Darby, Alan Johnson, Charles "Chuck D." Davis, Tyrone Frison, Roslyn Golden, Lenny Richard, Kevin Whittington, and Derrick Granberry.

Faith Fox, Kim Coles, and Lana Walker—when I needed shelter, safety, and food, you gave it. Angels you are.

My close "LA" Girlfriends: Jennifer Landry-Jackson, Nicole (Crockett) Pope, Alicia Procello-Maddox, Chandra (Simms) Mills, Denise Simms, Sheree Thompson, Sandy Mc Coy, Ashley Shaw, Kam Grey, and Robin Quincy— There are not enough words to describe what you have meant to me. Smiles, hugs, thanks, and lots of love.

Los Angeles Fellows: Howard Amos, Chip Washington, Teal Moss, David Mitchell, Gil Robertson, Mark Drummond, Butch Grimes, Julian Mosley, Bosko Kante,' Eddie Sly, Jr., Robert Ajakwe, Eddie Turner, Eddie Boles, and Yon Styles.

Am Rosen of Los Angeles is a visionary and has been my Naturopathy guru and herbalist for many, many years. I met Am through one of my closest friends, the late Allison Fisher. He helped her to become healthy through natural treatments, herbs, and remedies for several years, after she had been treated by western medicine for breast cancer. I miss Allison, and I love Am for his expertise in spurring the restoration of health. He is *extraordinary* and deep, and I am grateful for his works with me.

Portland Friends: Vanessa Gaston, Danielle and Otto Burston, Rebecca Star Livingston, and Lou Radja— the time of my Northwestern life was meeting you.

East Coast/DC Good Friends: Andrea Sorey, Antoinette Sykes, Darin Kenley, Diallo Sumbry, Rae Anne Gordon, Kym Jackson, Tony Bennae Richard, and Hillari Hawkins— Thank you for all that you are and all that you do. May each of you continue to be blessed as you continue to build and share your time and talents.

Nicole Cleveland, you teach people how to live through your example and through your publication, breatheagainmagazine. com. You stood in the gap and helped me to understand the value and necessity of utilizing 21st Century tools like Facebook, Twitter and the like. I admire you; I appreciate you; and I thank you for showing women how much they matter through your considerable efforts. I also want to thank you from the bottom of my heart for introducing me to Corrie Petersen—thanks to her services at from VirtualFreedom4you.com, I have also become more efficient because of such great Virtual Assistant Support!

Summit Education in Florida helped me to find my footing as I was transitioning into my life's work(s)— as a person, leader, and servant.

I believe in the "Work," and I thank God and you for the "business" of transformation. Everybody "Gets to Go!" Ralph Campbell, Ken and Kathy Cushman; FL108 Jay Caputo, Dave Persichini, Rosebud Jarecki, "my buddy" Donna Connelly, "love princess" Beth Roberts, and "my sister" Monikah Ogando.

(Ms.) Daryle G. Brown is one of the kindest, brightest, most practical, and talented people I have ever met. There are no words to describe our friendship/sisterhood. All I can say is God answers prayer by placing people in our lives for seasons and reasons. Here's to a lifetime of continued stories, experiences, and joy…

My Unique Blended Family makes me "eldest sister" to a bunch of "siblings." I'm thankful to each of you and our parents for our big ole' family— Regina (Kevin), Chris, Jarrell (Andrea), Emily (Nick), Kenneth (Juanita), Alexis (Jody). Kelsi, you are a wonderful young woman and a great mom to my "big niece" Kiarah. I love you both so much. Finally, William… *"Poncho, Te quiero, mi hermano, Cisco!"*

Ministers: Rev. Johnnie Coleman, Founder of Universal Foundation for Better Living & Christ Universal Temple, Rev. Helen Carrey, and Rev. Evelyn Boyd; Rev. Della Reese Early Patricia Lett, Founder of Understanding Principles for Better Living Church, and Dr. Charles Brown; Pastor David Jefferson, Metropolitan Baptist Church; and Pastor F. James Clark, Founder of Shalom Church, City of Peace— Thank you for your willingness to do God's work and for your commitment to preaching and teaching Bible based principles and practices. In the name of Jesus, thank you for living in your *Extraordinary Purposes.*

"A friend loveth at all times, and a brother is born for adversity."
Proverbs 17:17

March 30, 2010 Addendum...
...Aunt Jerry

God has a way of working things out. I love and trust the Lord and, this morning my Aunt Jerry passed, unexpectedly. I'm still numb, as I haven't "made it back" to the home, we shared for many years—yet, I am honored and blessed to have known her and love her...I'm saying this to you because I was "waiting" until the book was printed before I shared the things I wrote about her...and I missed sharing it with her in her human life.

I have no more words other than to say, "Don't wait!" Please be about our Father's business—we need Him and He uses us to express and share. Things will not be perfect—and He uses us to express (press out) Good.

July 23, 1944—March 30, 2010
Rest in Peace my beloved aunt, Jerry Eileen (McHugh) Perry—I know you are looking down on us—and I pray you are smiling at Your legacy.

> *"She maketh fine linen, and selleth it; and delivereth girdles unto the merchant. Strength and honour are her clothing; and she shall rejoice in time to come. She openeth her mouth with wisdom; and in her tongue is the law of kindness. Her children arise up, and call her blessed; her husband also, and he praiseth her. Many daughters have done virtuously, but thou excellest them all. Favour is deceitful, and beauty is vain: but a woman that feareth the LORD, she shall be praised. Give her of the fruit of her hands; and let her own works praise her in the gates."*
> Proverbs 31:24–31

Appendix

Sermons from Young Ministers:

Brokenness: God's Equation to Fruitful Living! Minister Daryl E. Whittington

Introduction

Let's take our minds to 2,500 B.C. to Egypt in its glory. During these years, we see the Great Pyramids and many other wonders of the world. I believe the Egyptian dynasty was far superior to any other dynasty. For example, maps of the oceans and seas that the European countries discovered in 1600 A.D. were made by the Egyptians over 3,000 years before. They were masters of mathematics, physics, medicine, chemistry, botany, engineering, architecture, and sculpture—to name a few.

Imhotep, a middle class Egyptian, eventually became a statesman, a designer, a builder, and a physician. He became a close Vizier to Pharaoh. He is credited by some as being the first doctor, architect, and engineer—among many other titles. He performed the first successful brain surgery, removed a gall bladder and kidney stones, and invented the step pyramids. Imhotep used slaves or skilled workers (it is still a debate about who actually built the pyramids), who would often fall and injure themselves on the job. He observed that when these pyramid builders injured themselves, they would often suffer bone fractures. The bone fractures would heal improperly and often leave the victim crippled.

This caused Imhotep to take action, and he didn't disappoint. He found, if you have a broken limb that healed incorrectly, you could re-break the improperly healed bone and re-set the bone back into proper position and functional use of the limb.

In the Arabic culture, there is a term called "Jabr," with the root meaning the repairing of broken bones, and it is the root of a popular mathematic subject of today. Imhotep found that you could take something from a broken state to a more useful form. Thus birthing the beginning of what we call Algebra today.

We are just like those Great Pyramid builders; some of us are broken and don't even know it. The brokenness that I am talking about is "Sin." It totally pulls us away from the safety rails of God's Grace, and our decision to live apart from God causes us to fall and break spiritually, emotionally, and sometimes physically. Living apart from God is an equation for total brokenness, but "GOD HAS COME TO BALANCE THIS EQUATION!"

Through his son Jesus Christ, He takes us from where we are totally broken, but broken to His Will, to His direction, and to His purposes for our lives. He breaks us for a more useful service for what He has called us to do. God gave His best in His son Jesus with a great price to pay for our eternity. God has not called us to be broken forever, just until His plans and purposes for our seasonal troubles are accomplished. The purpose of this is that God is calling us unto Greatness and to a life of fruitful living.

Only when our will is broken, can others finally see that Jesus is shining through our cracks, our imperfections, and ineptitudes. Since we are a prepared people for a prepared place, others will see the true nature of our greatness and fruitful life styles. The source is

God Himself. God allows His children to be broken for a purpose that is much bigger than our personal goals, our dreams, and any accomplishment. It is for His glory! And at the right time, in our broken state, He will exalt us in this world and/or the greater world to come.

- The equation of God's Greatness and to fruitful living lies in brokenness is probably best represented in the biblical character of Joseph.

Proposition: Brokenness is God's Equation to Greatest and Fruitful Living!

Main Point 1: Brokenness shows if we really are what we claim to be.

- What does it mean to be broken?
    - The Lord Jesus tells us in John 12, *"except the grain of Wheat falling into the ground die, it abides alone; but if it dies, it bears much fruit."* Life is in the grain of wheat, but there is a shell, if not split open, the wheat cannot grow.
    - "Except the grain of wheat falling into the ground die...." what is this death? It is the cracking open of the shell through the working together of temperature, humidity, etc. in the soil. Once the shell is split open, the wheat begins to grow. So the question here is not whether there is life within but whether the outside shell is cracked open!" We are like the grain of wheat as believers, that when we are broken, the Holy Spirit just shines through our imperfections and we are made stronger by our imperfections of life.

- What is the purpose of spiritual brokenness?
    o   For God to have His glory shine through our life.

- It is imperative that the outward shell, as a believer, be broken to receive God's best.
    o   We have to die to self ego, self will (keyword "SELF")

Main Point 2: Brokenness is the equation to true Restoration.

- We learn that God's Way is the best way.
    o   Only when we come to the end of ourselves can we learn to experience God's best.

- (Mathew 11:28–29) *Jesus said Come unto me, all that labor and are heavy laden, and I shall give you rest, take my yoke about me and learn from me, for I am gentle and humble in heart, and you will find rest for your souls.*
    o   Jesus is simply saying…bring me your brokenness; bring me your broken dreams, broken families, addictions, rejections from a parents, broken faith, all of your hurts and pains and difficulties in life, and that thing that happened to you when you were as a little boy or a little girl….And know that I am God! And only I can put it together again, and only I can make you whole. Only I can restore you; and, His promises are conditional.

- God allows us to be broken to the extent of His power.
    o   When we are truly broken, we…in our salvation will not have any part to boast about. We will have no glory in our restoration, and only God will get 100% of the glory. Only God brought you through this difficult season.

Main Point 3: Brokenness teaches us the wisdom to unlock Fruitful Life and Greatness.

- Brokenness produces a special type of Character.
    - Humility, a total 100% dependence on the LORD for everything, wise money management, perseverance, etc.

- Brokenness prepares from the Pit to the Palace.
    - With character, which has been tried by fire, we learn how to receive God's blessing and be godly stewards over whatever he gives us.
    - He developed a close fellowship and powerful prayer life.

- Greatness costs.
    - Everyone wants to have a flat six-pack stomach. But, very few people are truly willing to do what is required to get the flat stomach. Greatness will sometimes cost you everything.

Conclusion:

Meet Joseph:

- There is more written about Joseph in the book of Genesis, than is Abraham, the "father of faith," or the greatest catastrophic event in human history, the Great Flood.

- There are more writings about Joseph than Isaac, or Jacob.

- He wasn't perfect or sinless, but no sin is recorded in scripture.

- Joseph is the final of the 7 "great men" of Genesis.

- God broke Joseph to save the children of Israel and other surrounding great nations from a great famine.

In chapters 37–40 of Genesis, there are 3 Examples of Joseph's Brokenness.

[1] First, he was betrayed by his brothers and sold into slavery.

[2] Second, he was falsely accused by Potiphar's wife and thrown into prison.

[3] Third, he was forgotten in prison by the King's Cupbearer.

Finally, God allowed Joseph to endure many trials that challenged Joseph's faith, testimony, integrity, and prayer life. God blessed Joseph with the ability to interpret dreams. This was only accomplished because Joseph knew one thing, he could not interpret the dreams apart from God, and that only God can truly interpret the dreams. Finally, at the end of the story, God allows Joseph to sit before Pharaoh (Who was a pagan worshipper), and Joseph interprets the dream of Pharaoh, which saved all of Egypt and preserved the lineage of the children of Israel, from which Christ was born. Joseph who was sold into slavery by his brothers, was falsely accused by Potiphar's wife, and thrown in jail.

While in Jail, the King's Cupbearer, made an agreement with Joseph to tell the Pharaoh that Joseph was innocent. However, when he got out of prison, the cupbearer forgot about the agreement. Still, Joseph never loses his integrity or faith and only grows closer to the Lord. This man spent over 13 years in prison and slavery, until God allowed Joseph to sit in front of Pharaoh because none of Pharaoh's wise men could interpret Pharaoh's dream. After he interpreted the dream of Pharaoh, he was promoted to 2nd in charge of all the affairs of Egypt, and Joseph only answered to Pharaoh. God exalted Joseph at the proper time not only to save Joseph, but many lineages of people.

God wasn't done yet. The Bible tells us the reason why Joseph named his first child Manasseh—whose name means, "God has made me forget all my hardship and all my father's household." God restored Joseph life's to greatness beyond anyone's wildest imagination and even healed Joseph's memory of his pain and suffering.

Joseph named the 2nd son Ephraim "...for God hath made me fruitful in the land of my affliction." We see that in the midst of great trails and tribulation we can still produce godly fruit. Everyone connected to Joseph was blessed. Joseph through a 13-year long extreme season of brokenness, saw God was/is still faithful, and we can have the confidence to endure anything in life. The Christian life is not about what we can NOT do or what we must abstain from, but the Christian life is about what we CAN do! We have power to do endure anything and overcome the most difficult circumstances!

Sermons from Young Ministers:

"Hope for the Hurting"
Words of Pastor Cedric Portis

Third Presbyterian Church
1/10/2010

Luke 13:10–17 (NIV)

On a Sabbath Jesus was teaching in one of the synagogues, and a woman was there who had been crippled by a spirit for eighteen years. She was bent over and could not straighten up at all. When Jesus saw her, he called her forward and said to her, "Woman, you are set free from your infirmity." Then he put his hands on her, and immediately she straightened up and praised God. Indignant because Jesus had healed on the Sabbath, the synagogue ruler said to the people, "There are six days for work. So come and be healed on those days, not on the Sabbath." The Lord answered him, "You hypocrites! Doesn't each of you on the Sabbath untie his ox or donkey from the stall and lead it out to give it water? Then should not this woman, a daughter of Abraham, whom Satan has kept bound for eighteen long years, be set free on the Sabbath day from what bound her?" When he said this, all his opponents were humiliated, but the people were delighted with all the wonderful things he was doing.

There are two types of people in the world: those who have been hurt and those who will be hurt. We can't escape it, nor can we avoid it. Furthermore, there is a fallacy, that when we make a commitment to follow Christ, that we receive an exemption from getting hurt; and that could not be further from the truth. We should not despair in light of this reality because Jesus offers hope for those who are hurting.

Jesus Cares for Hurting People.

This woman was not oblivious to Jesus; He was not indifferent to her pain. Notice that there is no indication that this woman calls out to Jesus; on the contrary, it is Jesus who calls to the woman in the midst of her pain. And, that is how it is….it is God who awakes us, calls us, and makes us alive in our dead situation.

Jesus reached out to her in the same way that He reaches out to us, in the midst of our pain…In the midst of a storm we tend to get extremely vexed in our spirit because we feel abandoned, alone…. no one understands, no one cares about me in my situations….but Jesus our high priest.

Hebrews 4:14–16

Therefore, since we have a great high priest who has gone through the heavens, Jesus the Son of God, let us hold firmly to the faith we profess. For we do not have a high priest who is unable to sympathize with our weaknesses, but we have one who has been tempted in every way, just as we are—yet was without sin. Let us then approach the throne of grace with confidence, so that we may receive mercy and find grace to help us in our time of need.

If we look throughout the New Testament, Jesus always focused on the marginalized, outcasts; the women, prostitutes, widows, tax collectors, lepers…therefore, Jesus, not only understands what we are going though, but is going through it with us…He is reaching out to you today in whatever situation you may be facing. Don't ever think that Jesus is not aware of your situation or unmoved by your tears. You may not understand many things that you are going through or why your prayers go unanswered, but you can be confident that God knows and cares about your pain.

Servants take on the characteristics of their master, and, as servants of the Lord Jesus, we too should notice the hurting and respond to their need. We are not to be so caught up in ourselves and the world that we lose our Master's perspective. If we begin to look at people and their situation as Jesus does, we will have the compassion needed to really impact the lives of others with the Gospel message; we will begin to pray for the hurting and use the resources that God has blessed us with to edify.

Jesus is showing us here how to be difference makers, and we must start to do that with genuine concern for the marginalized, outcast, oppressed, less fortunate—those who are in physical, as well as spiritual bondage. Do you know that's why we harp so much on Bible Study and Sunday School?

God is teaching us how to be TRAINED RESPONDERS…if you're in an accident and the EMS worker shows up to the crash scene and just looks at you and replies, "Whew, bad accident, huh? You're pretty messed up, aren't you? I just don't know if you're going to make it."

And your response would be, "Hey….I'm definitely not going to make it, if you don't do something….Why are you driving this truck, if you can't do anything; why are you carrying that medical bag; if you can't do anything…Why are you wearing that uniform, if you can't do anything……"

Church, this is how we look when we refuse to study the word of God, ignore the training that is made possible through Sunday school and Bible study…We show up to the emotional accidents; the emotional train wrecks among our family members, friends and co-workers and we stand there like an untrained EMS worker saying…"Whew…bad accident….whew, you're pretty messed up, aren't you…I don't know if you're going to make it." And the person looking at you may not say it, but if they knew, better they would say…"I'm definitely not going to make it with you just telling me what I already know…." You mean to tell me you go to church every week and that's all you can say? Why are you carrying that Bible, if you don't even take the time to read what's in it?

Church, what are we here to do? We are here for training (so) that, when we show up to these emotional train wrecks we react to the situation like this….." Ma'am, be still. You may feel like a victim, but I am about to show you how to be victorious"…."Sir, you may be oppressed, but allow me show you how to be an over-comer…."You may be depressed and dejected, but my training is such that I am about to show you how to be (blessed)."

Jesus rebuked those who ignored hurting people. This religious leader was more focused on religious rules and maintaining the order of service, than in ministering to hurting people. He had no joy, no praise, and no relief at this woman's healing. Jesus was greatly angered by this uncaring, indifferent response.

In the rat race that many of us are running, we should not get so focused on the cheese…that the others who have fallen in the race are of no consequence to us. If you are not helping someone to the finish line, then what good is it to be at the finish line alone and unfulfilled? We need to stop and help, not proceed with everyday life in hypocritical indifference.

And we have talked about this is in Bible School, the fact that we live in what I call a microwave society; this means, that when there is a problem, we just want it gone right now.

This is where we get the idea that, if we just throw money at a situation, it will disappear or at least ease our conscience that we have done something. Remember this…most of the time money may stop the apparent bleeding, but the wound is still in need of stitches. We have to look beyond the immediate circumstances and see if God is using us to heal the hurt. Someone may need to talk; they may need some compassion; they may just need to know that someone cares about them in their situation, and that's what Jesus is training us to do today.

Jesus Is Powerful Enough To Heal Hurting People

If all Jesus had was compassion to offer to our situation of hurt, then it would not be much of a consolation because our situation would still be hopeless. But this is not the case; Jesus does not only offer compassion but healing for your hurts, deliverance from your bondage, and calm to your storm. Remember this: there is nothing you can or ever will face that is bigger or more powerful than God. You may have suffered for many years as this woman did, but you can still be hopeful. There is hope because there is Jesus. He set this woman free from her infirmity, and He can set you free from yours. Never ever, give up hope! No matter what type of problem, hurt, or bondage you may be facing because you serve a God who is with you in your situation and who can deliver you from your situation.

If you are physically sick, He can heal you.

If your family is troubled, He can restore it.

If your home life is falling apart, He can renovate it.

If you marriage seems dead, He can revive it.

If your children have gone astray, He can retrieve them.

If you are not saved, let Him renew you.

There is nothing beyond the power of Jesus Christ. I know some of you may have been hurting for a long time, and you have lost hope. I know some of you no longer really expect Jesus to supernaturally intervene in your situation or need.

I know many of you have questions of God, and I cannot answer every question you may have; nevertheless, I do encourage you to look at this story to renew your faith and expectations. Let your faith be strengthened by God's Word. Keep your hope alive because Jesus still heals the hurting.

Isaiah 40:28–31

Do you not know? Have you not heard? The Lord is the everlasting God, the Creator of the ends of the earth. He will not grow tired or weary, and his understanding no one can fathom. He gives strength to the weary and increases the power of the weak. Even youths grow tired and weary, and young men stumble and fall; but those who hope in the Lord will renew their strength. They will soar on wings like eagles; they will run and not grow weary, they will walk and not be faint.

There are Christians today who no longer pray for healing because they have lost their faith and don't think God will heal them. There are Christians today whose marriages are failing, yet they have no real expectation for Jesus to restore their marriage because they think it is too late. There are people who have quit serving in ministry out of discouragement because they think their situation is beyond God's help. Our thinking needs to change, if it is like this. God wants to work miracles in your life….do we believe that Jesus is powerful enough to heal our hurts.

Jesus Explains That Satan, Not God, Is The Cause of Hurting People.

When people are suffering the natural response is to slip in the pity party zone of "Why me?" "God, why are you putting me through this?" "Why did God give me cancer; why did God take my child and on, and on, and on..."

We erroneously assume that God must be behind all of the hurting we experience, and this must be part of his divine plan...question for us this morning...How can we have hope in a God we feel is responsible for our hurting? Jesus explains that it is not God but Satan that has kept this woman bound. Job lost all his children, all his possessions, and his entire body had been attacked with sores, and the Bible says that in all these things Job sinned not nor charged God foolishly. When we blame God for all the "bad" things that happen....these are foolish charges against God. The Bible teaches us that Satan is the one who brought pain, suffering, and sorrow into the world through sin. God created the world *good!* Look at the ministry of Jesus. Much of His ministry was spent healing and easing the suffering of people. Jesus looked upon death and diseases as intruders and aliens in God's world.

I find it rather strange that people both believers and non-believers turn, shaking a clinched fist to God when things go wrong in their life; but, when it comes to God asking why were you knowingly disobedient to my Will, we want to quote the late Flip Wilson and respond, "The devil made me do it." A couple of things should be noted here to prevent misunderstandings. First, I do believe as the Bible teaches, that God uses the hurts and pains of life for good purposes. Satan may be behind the hurting, but God can take what Satan intended for evil and use it for good.

Romans 8:28

And we know that all things work together for good to them that love God, to them who are the called according to his purpose.

Having said that, I want to emphasize, that in the majority of cases, the Bible tells us that Satan is directly or indirectly the explanation for the troubles, pains, and hurts of this world. This is good news and reason for those who are hurting to have hope because it means that God is not against us, rather He is for us.

Romans 8:31

What shall we then say to these things? If God be for us, who can be against us?

I want to point out that nothing in this text indicates that this woman was demon possessed or demonized. No demon manifested itself, was rebuked, or cast out for this reason. In fact, in verse 14 the religious leader says that she was "healed" not delivered, and Jesus specifically says in verse 12 that she was "set free from her infirmity (sickness, disease)." I say all this to point out that while a genuine Christian cannot be possessed by a demon, they can be attacked by Satan in their bodies, marriages, ministries, finances, etc.

John 10:28–29

And I give unto them eternal life; and they shall never perish, neither shall any man pluck them out of my hand. My Father, which gave them me, is greater than all; and no man is able to pluck them out of my Father's hand.

When these attacks come, we need to recognize the source of the attacks and go to Jesus for healing and strength in His mighty power. *God has brought you here today as conformation that you are special,* to give you hope, to let you know healing comes from Him....Let us pray...

Recommended Resources from
Dr. Lee Roy Jefferson

George Barna. <u>The Power of Vision</u>, Regal Books, Ventura, CA.

Bill Bright. <u>A Handbook for Christian Maturity</u>, New Life Publication, A Ministry of Campus Crusade.

Loren Broadus. <u>How to Stop Procrastinating & Start Living</u>, Augsburg Publishing House, Minneapolis, MN.

Jim Collins. <u>Good to Great, Harper Business</u>, New York, NY.

Steven Collins. <u>Christian Discipleship, Hensley Publishing</u>. Tulsa, OK.

A.K. Shamsid-Deen. <u>Power Speaking for Self-Empowerment.</u> Shamsid-Deen Marketing Services, Elizabeth, NJ.

Robert Fulghum. <u>All I Really Need to Know I Learned In Kindergarten</u>, Villard Books, New York.

Howard G. Hendricks & William D. Hendricks. <u>Living by the Book</u>. Moody Press, Chicago, IL.

Howard Hendricks. <u>Teaching to Change Lives</u>, Multnomah Publishers, A Division of Random House.

Malcolm Kushner. <u>Public Speaking for Dummies</u>, Wiley Publishing, Inc., Indianapolis, IN.

Fred R. Lybrand. <u>Preaching On Your Feet</u>, Academic, Nashville, TN.

George O. McCalep. <u>Faithful Over a few Things</u>, Orman Press, Lithonia, GA.

George O. McCalep. <u>Sin In The House</u>, Orman Press, Lithonia, GA.

Lora-Ellen McKinney. <u>Christian Education in the African American Church</u>, Judson Press, Valley Forge, PA.

Mike Nappa. <u>Who Moved My Church</u>, River Oak Publishing, Tulsa, OK.

Stephen F. Olford with David Olford. <u>Anointed Expository Preaching,</u> Broadman & Holman Publisher, Nashville, TN.

Mary K. Sellon & Daniel P. Smith. <u>Practicing Right Relationship</u>, The Alban Institute, Herndon, VA.

Quick Order Form

If you really liked this book, tell a friend, or buy a copy for them:

Buy "If You Really Want to Live,
Be Extraordinary! TODAY!

Web: www.jolenajohnson.com
Email: books@absolutegood.com

We accept all major credit cards through PayPal:

c/o Absolute Good Training & Life Skills Management

Call or email today for checks, money orders, or
for quantity discounts. 240.644.2500

Name & Title _____

Organization _____

Address _____

City/State/Zip _____

Phone _____

E-mail _____

Please send me FREE Information on
☐ Books ☐ Speaking ☐ Training ☐ Seminar
☐ Good Projects Together

Please send me copies of "*If You Really Want to Live, Be Extraordinary!*" for $24.95 each and $4.00 for shipping and handling. Please call for quantity discounts. Published by Mission Possible Press in conjunction with Absolute Good Training & Life Skills Management. THANK YOU!

To

Ruth Walker
" Daughter "

From

Bessie Walker

" Mom "

Breinigsville, PA USA
11 December 2010
251179BV00001B/5/P